DAVID EDGAR

David Edgar was born into a theatre family and took up writing full time in 1972. In 1989, he founded Britain's first graduate playwriting course, at the University of Birmingham, of which he was director for ten years. His stage adaptations include Albie Sachs's *Jail Diary*, Robert Louis Stevenson's *Dr Jekyll and Mr Hyde*, Charles Dickens's *Nicholas Nickleby* and Charles Dickens's *A Christmas Carol* (all for the Royal Shakespeare Company), Gitta Sereny's biography of *Albert Speer* (National Theatre) and Julian Barnes's *Arthur & George* (Birmingham Repertory Theatre), as well as translations of Bertolt Brecht's *Galileo* (Birmingham Repertory Theatre), Brecht's *Mother Courage and Her Children* (Shakespeare Festival, Stratford, Ontario) and Henrik Ibsen's *The Master Builder* (Chichester Festival Theatre). He has written two community plays for Dorchester: *Entertaining Strangers* and *A Time to Keep* (with Stephanie Dale). His revised version of *Entertaining Strangers* was presented at the National Theatre, as were *The Shape of the Table* and *Playing with Fire*. In addition to *Maydays*, his original plays for the RSC include *Destiny*, *Pentecost*, *The Prisoner's Dilemma* and *Written on the Heart*. Other recent plays include *Daughters of the Revolution* and *Mothers Against* (Oregon Shakespeare Festival and Berkeley Repertory Theatre), *Testing the Echo* (Out of Joint) and *If Only* (Minerva Theatre, Chichester). He is the author of *How Plays Work*.

David Edgar

MAYDAYS & TRYING IT ON

NICK HERN BOOKS
London
www.nickhernbooks.co.uk

ABOUT THE ROYAL SHAKESPEARE COMPANY

The Shakespeare Memorial Theatre opened in Stratford-upon-Avon in 1879. Since then the plays of Shakespeare have been performed here, alongside the work of his contemporaries and of living modern playwrights. In 1960, the Royal Shakespeare Company was formed, gaining its Royal Charter in 1961. The founding principles of the Company were threefold: the Company would embrace the freedom and power of Shakespeare's work, train and develop young actors and directors and, crucially, experiment in new ways of making theatre. The RSC quickly became known for exhilarating performances of Shakespeare alongside new masterpieces such as *The Homecoming* and *Old Times* by Harold Pinter. It was a combination that thrilled audiences and this close and exacting relationship between writers from different eras has become the fuel that powers the creativity of the RSC.

In 1974, The Other Place opened in a tin hut on Waterside under the visionary leadership and artistic directorship of Buzz Goodbody. Determined to explore Shakespeare's plays in intimate proximity to her audience and to make small-scale, radical new work, Buzz revitalised the Company's interrogation between the contemporary and classical repertoire. Reopened in 2016 under the artistic directorship of Erica Whyman, The Other Place is once again the home for experimentation and the development of exciting new ideas.

In our 55 years of producing new plays, we have collaborated with some of the most exciting writers of their generation. These have included: Edward Albee, Howard Barker, Alice Birch, Richard Bean, Edward Bond, Howard Brenton, Marina Carr, Caryl Churchill, Martin Crimp, Can Dündar, David Edgar, Helen Edmundson, James Fenton, Georgia Fitch, Fraser Grace, David Greig, Tanika Gupta, Matt Hartley, Ella Hickson, Kirsty Housley, Dennis Kelly, Anders Lustgarten, Tarell Alvin McCraney, Martin McDonagh, Tom Morton-Smith, Rona Munro, Richard Nelson, Anthony Neilson, Harold Pinter, Phil Porter, Mike Poulton, Mark Ravenhill, Somalia Seaton, Adriano Shaplin, Tom Stoppard, debbie tucker green, Frances Ya-Chu Cowhig, Timberlake Wertenbaker, Peter Whelan and Roy Williams.

The Company today is led by Gregory Doran, whose appointment as Artistic Director represents a long-term commitment to the disciplines and craftsmanship required to put on the plays of Shakespeare. The RSC under his leadership is committed to illuminating the relevance of Shakespeare's plays and the works of his contemporaries for the next generation of audiences and believes that our continued investment in new plays and living writers is an essential part of that mission.

The RSC is grateful for the significant support of its principal funder, Arts Council England, without which our work would not be possible. Around 75 per cent of the RSC's income is self-generated from Box Office sales, sponsorship, donations, enterprise and partnerships with other organisations.

Supported using public funding by
**ARTS COUNCIL
ENGLAND**

NEW WORK AT THE RSC

We are a contemporary theatre company built on classical rigour. Through an extensive programme of research and development, we resource writers, directors and actors to explore and develop new ideas for our stages, and as part of this we commission playwrights to engage with the muscularity and ambition of the classics and to set Shakespeare's world in the context of our own.

We invite writers to spend time with us in our rehearsal rooms, with our actors and creative teams. Alongside developing new plays for all our stages, we invite playwrights to contribute dramaturgically to both our productions of Shakespeare and his contemporaries, as well as our work for, and with, young people. We believe that engaging with living writers and contemporary theatre-makers helps to establish a creative culture within the Company which both inspires new work and creates an ever more urgent sense of enquiry into the classics.

Shakespeare was a great innovator and breaker of rules, as well as a bold commentator on the times in which he lived. It is his spirit which informs new work at the RSC. Erica Whyman, Deputy Artistic Director, heads up this strand of the Company's work alongside Pippa Hill as Literary Manager.

The work of the RSC Literary Department is generously supported by
THE DRUE HEINZ TRUST.

Maydays by David Edgar was first presented at the Barbican Theatre, London on 13 October 1985.

This revised and updated version of the play was presented as part of the autumn 2018 Mischief Festival at The Other Place, Stratford-upon-Avon, on 27 September 2018. The cast was as follows:

PUGACHEV/TRELAWNEY/CHORUS	**GEOFFREY BEEVERS**
WEINER/MRS GLASS/WOMAN/CHORUS	**GILLIAN BEVAN**
JEREMY/SKURATOV/CHORUS	**RICHARD CANT**
CLARA/JUDY/CHORUS	**SOPHIE KHAN LEVY**
PHIL/KOROLENKO/CHORUS	**CHRIS NAYAK**
AMANDA/ERICA/CHORUS	**LILY NICHOL**
MARTIN/CHORUS	**MARK QUARTLEY**
JAMES GRAIN/PALOCZI/CHORUS	**CHRISTOPHER SIMPSON**
BRYONY/MOLLY/TANYA/CHORUS	**LIYAH SUMMERS**
LERMONTOV/CHORUS	**JAY TAYLOR**

The RSC Acting Companies are generously supported by THE GATSBY CHARITABLE FOUNDATION and THE KOVNER FOUNDATION.

Director	**Owen Horsley**
Designer	**Simon Wells**
Lighting Designer	**Claire Gerrens**
Sound Designer	**Steven Atkinson**
Movement Director	**Polly Bennett**
Company Voice and Text Work	**Kate Godfrey**
Assistant Director	**Rosa Crompton**
Casting Director	**Matthew Dewsbury**
Dramaturg	**Pippa Hill**
Production Manager	**Julian Cree**
Costume Supervisor	**Samantha Pickering**
Props Supervisor	**Charlotte King**
Company Stage Manager	**Julia Wade**
Assistant Stage Manager	**PK Thummukgool**
Producer	**Claire Birch**
Crew	**Dan Avery**
	Samantha Gray
	Alex Hughes
	Jon Lawrence
	Laura O'Driscoll
	Matty Sanders

The historical timeline displayed in the foyer is based on research by the company during rehearsals.
This text may differ slightly from the play as performed.

LOVE THE RSC?

Become a Member or Patron and support our work

The RSC is a registered charity. Our aim is to stage theatre at its best, made in Stratford-upon-Avon and shared around the world with the widest possible audience and we need your support.

Become an RSC Member from £50 per year and access up to three weeks of Priority Booking, advance information, exclusive discounts and special offers, including free on-the-day seat upgrades.

Or support as a Patron from £150 per year for up to one additional week of Priority Booking, plus enjoy opportunities to discover more through special behind-the-scenes events.

For more information visit **rsc.org.uk/support** or call the RSC Membership Office on 01789 403440.

THE ROYAL SHAKESPEARE COMPANY

CAST

GEOFFREY BEEVERS
PUGACHEV/TRELAWNEY/CHORUS
RSC: *The Heresy of Love, Measure for Measure, A Servant to Two Masters, Pericles, Henry VIII, The Comedy of Errors, Mother Courage, The Time of Your Life, Red Star, The Devils.*
THIS SEASON: *Maydays.*
TRAINED: LAMDA.
THEATRE INCLUDES: *Amadeus, Playing with Fire, The UN Inspector, The Winter's Tale* (National Theatre); *The Audience* (Broadway); *Hamlet, The Antipodes* (Shakespeare's Globe); *War and Peace, A Passage to India* (Shared Experience); *Hamlet, A Midsummer Night's Dream, The Tempest, King Lear* (in the USA); *A Bequest to the Nation, Dandy Dick, Eurydice, The Audience* (West End).
TELEVISION INCLUDES: *Holby City, The Tudors, Silent Witness, Inspector Morse, Sherlock Holmes, Poirot, Casualty, Yes Prime Minister, Red Dwarf, Measure for Measure, Doctor Who, A Very British Coup, The Jewel in the Crown.*
RADIO INCLUDES: Many plays for BBC; audiobooks; The Master in *Doctor Who* spin-offs.
FILM INCLUDES: *Victor/Victoria, The Woodlanders, Miss Potter.* Geoffrey also writes and directs, including *Adam Bede* (Time Out Award), and *The Middlemarch Trilogy* for the Orange Tree Theatre. He has published two novels.

GILLIAN BEVAN
WEINER/MRS GLASS/WOMAN/CHORUS
RSC: Title role in *Cymbeline* (Stratford/ Barbican, London), Dorothy in *The Wizard of Oz*, Celia in *As You Like It*.
THIS SEASON: *Maydays.*
TRAINED: Central School of Speech and Drama.
THEATRE INCLUDES: Polonia in *Hamlet* (MTA Best Supporting Actress), Mrs Lovett in *Sweeney Todd*, The Witch in *Into the Woods* (Royal Exchange); Mrs Wilkinson in *Billy Elliot* (West End. Laurence Olivier Audience Award 2013); *The Last Days of Troy* (Shakespeare's Globe); Mama Mizner in *Road Show* (Menier Chocolate Factory); 80th birthday tribute concert of *Company* (Donmar Warehouse); *My Fair Lady* (Teatro San Carlo Opera House, Naples); Sheila in *Relatively Speaking* (Newbury Watermill); Alice in *Billy Liar* (West Yorkshire Playhouse); Raffaella in *Grand Hotel* (Donmar Warehouse); *On Your Toes* (Japan tour). Gillian started work at Perth Rep, then worked with rep companies including the Bristol Old Vic and Alan Ayckbourn's Theatre-in-the-Round, with whom she appeared in *Season's Greetings, Me, Myself and I, Making Tracks, Saturday, Sunday, Monday, Twelfth Night* and a US tour of *Way Upstream* and *Absent Friends.*

Gillian was a founder member of Tight Assets Theatre with Tessa Peake-Jones and Helen Kluger.

TELEVISION INCLUDES: Gina Hope in *Holby City*, Claire Hunter in *Teachers*, Screen One drama *Ghostwatch*, Theresa May in *The Windsors*, *The Innocents*, *Lewis*, Det Supt Penfold in *The Chief*, Cissie in *Lost Empires, A Touch of Frost, Foyle's War, Peak Practice, Loved by You, New Tricks*.

FILM INCLUDES: *London Road*, film of Royal Exchange's *Hamlet*, RSC Live From *Cymbeline, Sergeant Slaughter, Maigret*.

RADIO INCLUDES: Directed *John Dodd Gets Taken for a Ride* and *A Good Place for Fishing* (Radio 4); co-wrote Radio 5's *Fifteen Love*; co-wrote/produced Radio 4's *No Rights - Only Wrongs*; performed in many plays and readings for BBC Radio 4.

RICHARD CANT
JEREMY/SKURATOV/CHORUS
RSC: *Cymbeline, Hamlet, Much Ado About Nothing.*
THIS SEASON: *Maydays.*
TRAINED: Central School of Speech and Drama.

THEATRE INCLUDES: *Saint Joan* (Donmar Warehouse); *Stella* (Lift/Brighton Festival); *Medea* (Almeida); *My Night with Reg* (Donmar Warehouse/Apollo Theatre); *The Trial* (Young Vic); *War Horse* (NT at New London Theatre); *Salome* (Headlong); *Troilus and Cressida, Cymbeline, As You Like It* (Cheek by Jowl); *Original Sin, The Country Wife* (Sheffield Crucible); *Other People* (Royal Court); *Pera Pelas* (Gate); *She Stoops To Conquer* (New Kent Opera); *Angels in America* (Manchester Library Theatre); *The Canterbury Tales* (Garrick); *Love's Labour's Lost* (Ipswich Wolsey); *Waterland* (Eastern Angles).

TELEVISION INCLUDES: *Silent Witness, Taboo, Mapp and Lucia, Outlander, Vexed, Above Suspicion – The Red Dahlia, Doctors, The Bill, Doctor Who, Bleak House, Ian Fleming – Bond Maker, Midsomer Murders, Gunpowder, Treason & Plot, Shackleton, The Way We Live Now, Gimme Gimme Gimme, This Life, The Day Today.*

FILM INCLUDES: *Mary Queen of Scots, Stan and Ollie, Sparkle, (Past Present Future) Imperfect, The Lawless Heart.*

RADIO/AUDIO INCLUDES: *Medieval Hitchhiker, Assassin's Creed III* and *IV, 007 Legends.*

SOPHIE KHAN LEVY
CLARA/JUDY/CHORUS
RSC: *A Midsummer Night's Dream*
(RSC/Garsington Opera), *The Christmas
Truce, Love's Labour's Lost, Love's
Labour's Won.*
THIS SEASON: *Maydays.*
TRAINED: Guildhall School of Music
and Drama.
THEATRE INCLUDES: *Hanna* (Arcola/
tour); *Fracked!* (Chichester Festival
Theatre/tour/Yvonne Arnaud Theatre/
Jonathan Church Productions); *Cymbeline*
(Phizzical Productions).

CHRIS NAYAK
PHIL/KOROLENKO/CHORUS
RSC: *A Midsummer Night's Dream:
A Play for the Nation, A Midsummer
Night's Dream* (RSC/Garsington Opera),
*Much Ado About Nothing, Love's
Labour's Lost, Love's Labour's Won,
The Christmas Truce.*
THIS SEASON: *Maydays.*
TRAINED: Bristol Old Vic Theatre School.
THEATRE INCLUDES: *King Lear*
(Shakespeare's Globe); *There or Here*
(Park Theatre); *Anita and Me* (Stratford
East); *The Wind in the Willows, Arthur
and George, East is East* (Birmingham
Rep); *Invasion!* (Soho Theatre); *Macbeth*
(Little Angel Theatre); *Leaving Planet Earth*
(Edinburgh International Festival);
A Passage to India (Shared Experience);
*She Stoops to Conquer, The League of
Youth* (Nottingham Playhouse); *Lisa's
Sex Strike, Romeo and Juliet* (Northern
Broadsides); *Stand Up Diggers All*
(Pentabus); *Indian Ink* (Salisbury
Playhouse); *The Marriage of Figaro*
(Tara Arts); *East is East* (York Theatre
Royal); *Mother Goose and the Wolf*
(Greenwich Theatre); *Punchkin: Enchanter*
(London Bubble).
TELEVISION INCLUDES: *The Job Lot,
Coronation Street, Doctors, Primeval,
Love Soup, Casualty, Judge John Deed,
The Bill.*
RADIO INCLUDES: Series 1 and 2 of *Bindi
Business, Letters from a Young Indian
Revolutionary.*

LILY NICHOL
AMANDA/ERICA/CHORUS
RSC: *Imperium I* and *II.*
THIS SEASON: *Maydays.*
TRAINED: Arts Educational Schools London.
THEATRE INCLUDES: *If We Were Older* (National Theatre New Views); *Julius Caesar* (Sheffield Crucible); *Those Who Trespass* (HighTide); *Table, As You Like It, Machinal* (ArtsEd); *179 Hackney Road* (Bridge Theatre Company).
FILM INCLUDES: *Mary Jane* (RSA/Blackdog Films), *Intimacy* (short).

MARK QUARTLEY
MARTIN/CHORUS
RSC: *The Tempest* **(Stratford/Barbican, London),** *Written on the Heart, Measure for Measure.*
THIS SEASON: *Maydays.*
TRAINED: RADA.
THEATRE INCLUDES: *Strife* (Chichester Festival Theatre); *Another Country, Macbeth* (Trafalgar Studios); *Ghosts* (Rose Theatre); *Private Peaceful* (National Theatre at Theatre Royal Haymarket); *The Tempest* (Theatre Royal Bath); *A Midsummer Night's Dream* (Shakespeare's Globe); *The War Has Not Yet Started* (Southwark Playhouse).
TELEVISION INCLUDES: *Shamed, Red Dwarf, Hoff the Record, In the Club, Lucky Man, Cuffs, Siblings, Vera.*
FILM INCLUDES: *Passenger, Otherwise Engaged, Love Pool.*
RADIO INCLUDES: *Something Understood, Private Peaceful, Not a Love Story, These Buttons We Wear.*

CHRISTOPHER SIMPSON
JAMES GRAIN/PALOCZI/CHORUS
RSC: *Pericles.*
THIS SEASON: *Maydays.*
THEATRE INCLUDES: *Brideshead Revisited* (York Theatre Royal/tour); *Forests* (international tour); *Leaner Faster Stronger* (part of the Cultural Olympiad at Sheffield Theatres); *The Knowledge, Little Platoons* (Bush); *Fallujah* (Truman's Brewery); *The Bacchae of Baghdad* (Abbey, Dublin); *Fragile Land* (Hampstead Theatre); *The Ramayana* (National Theatre); *Double Tongue* (Old Red Lion); *Off the Wall* (David Glass Ensemble); *Blue Remembered Hills* (Yellow Earth).
TELEVISION INCLUDES: *Shameless, All About George, State of Play, Second Generation, White Teeth.*
FILM INCLUDES: *Sixteen, The Day of the Flowers, It's a Wonderful Afterlife, Brick Lane, Mischief Night, Chromophobia, Code 46.*

LIYAH SUMMERS
BRYONY/MOLLY/TANYA/CHORUS
RSC DEBUT SEASON: *Maydays.*
TRAINED: Bristol Old Vic Theatre School.

THEATRE: This is Liyah's professional debut.
THEATRE WHILST TRAINING: Dorothy in *The Wizard of Oz*, Princess Alexandra/Chorus in *The Elephant Man* (Bristol Old Vic), Simone in *Been So Long*.

JAY TAYLOR
LERMONTOV/CHORUS
RSC: *Wolf Hall, Bring Up the Bodies* **(Stratford/West End/Broadway).**
THIS SEASON: *Maydays.*
TRAINED: RADA.
THEATRE INCLUDES: *Baskerville* (Liverpool Everyman); *46 Beacon, SH*TM*X* (Trafalgar); *Accolade* (St James Theatre); *Nell Gwyn* (Apollo Theatre/Shakespeare's Globe); *I Heart Peterborough* (Soho Theatre); *Joe/Boy* (The Last Refuge); *A Clockwork Orange* (Glasgow Citizens); *Troilus and Cressida, Titus Andronicus* (Shakespeare's Globe); *The Police* (The White Bear).
TELEVISION INCLUDES: *Manhunt, Britannia, Prime Suspect 1973, Silk, Tea Boys, Midsomer Murders, Misfits, Sirens, Consuming Passions, The Bill, The Fixer, Daphne, Holby City, EastEnders.*
FILM INCLUDES: *A Fantastic Fear of Everything, Donkey Punch, Red Tails, The Rise of the Footsoldier.*
RADIO: *The Russian Gambler.*

CREATIVE TEAM

STEVEN ATKINSON
SOUND DESIGNER
RSC: *Myth, The Earthworks, Fall of the Kingdom, Always Orange, King Lear (Associate Sound Designer)*. Steve is currently a member of the RSC Sound Department.
THIS SEASON: *Maydays*.
TRAINED: University of Huddersfield.
WORK INCLUDES: Following training, Steve worked for several years as a theatre technician and later as venue manager. In 2011 he joined the RSC Sound Department for the inaugural season in the redeveloped theatres. Since then he has toured for the RSC numerous times and installed residencies for RSC productions in Newcastle, the Roundhouse, the Barbican and the West End. In 2016 Steve took the *King & Country* season of shows to mainland China, the Hong Kong Arts Festival and the Brooklyn Academy of Music. In 2017 he returned to BAM as Associate Sound Designer on *King Lear*.
ART EXHIBITIONS: Sound design for *Interview (Prototype)* at The Lightbox, part of the Ingram Collection and Purchase Prize winner 2017; *Defence Cascade* at Compton Verney, private collection.

POLLY BENNETT
MOVEMENT DIRECTOR
RSC: *Salomé, A Midsummer Night's Dream, The Famous Victories of Henry V (tour); A Mad World My Masters*. Polly is an Associate Practitioner.
THIS SEASON: *Maydays*.
TRAINED: MA in Movement from the Royal Central School of Speech and Drama.
THEATRE INCLUDES: *The Village* (Theatre Royal Stratford East); *The Lehman Trilogy, The Great Wave, The Deep Blue Sea, Three Days in the Country, nut*

(National Theatre)*; As You Like It, To Kill a Mockingbird* (Regent's Park Open Air Theatre); *Travesties* (Menier Chocolate Factory/West End/Broadway); *Circle Mirror Transformation* (Manchester HOME); *People, Places and Things* (National Theatre/West End/UK tour/off-Broadway); *Touch, Blush* (Soho); Don Juan in *Soho* (Wyndham's); *Woyzeck* (Old Vic); *Junkyard* (Bristol Old Vic); *How My Light Is Spent, A Streetcar Named Desire* (Manchester Royal Exchange); *My Country: a work in progress* (National Theatre/UK tour); *Pomona* (National Theatre/Manchester Royal Exchange/Orange Tree); *Henry V* (Shanghai Dramatic Centre of Performing Arts); *Doctor Faustus* (Duke of York's); *The Maids* (Trafalgar Studios); *Yen, Plaques and Tangles, hang* (Royal Court); *The Lion, the Witch and the Wardrobe* (Birmingham Rep); *The Rise and Fall of Little Voice* (West Yorkshire Playhouse); *The Angry Brigade* (Bush); *Dunsinane* (National Theatre Scotland/US, Asia and UK tours); *The King's Speech* (Chichester/Birmingham Rep/UK tour).
FILM INCLUDES: *Bohemian Rhapsody* (Movement Coach), *The Little Stranger* (Choreographer), *Stan and Ollie* (Assistant Choreographer).
TELEVISION INCLUDES: *The Crown* series 3, *Killing Eve, Urban Myths, Gareth Malone's Best of British.*
OTHER: Assistant Movement Director on the London 2012 Olympics Opening Ceremony, Mass Cast Choreographer on the London 2012 Paralympic Opening Ceremony and Mass Cast Choreographer on Sochi Winter Olympics Opening and Paralympic Ceremonies 2014.
Polly is co-founder of The Mono Box.

ROSA CROMPTON

ASSISTANT DIRECTOR

RSC DEBUT SEASON: *Maydays.*
THEATRE INCLUDES: As Assistant/
Associate Director includes: *The Mentor*
(Vaudeville Theatre); *Raising Martha* (Park
Theatre); *Babe the Sheep Pig* (UK tour);
*Forever Yours Mary-Lou, The One That
Got Away* (Bath Ustinov); *Blithe Spirit*
(York Theatre Royal). As Director includes:
FCUK'D (Gilded Balloon); *Tits'n'Teeth*
(Underbelly); *Not Savages* (VAULT); *Siren*
(VAULT/Brasserie Zedel). Rosa directed
the NT Connections play *These Bridges*
for White City Youth Theatre at the Bush
Theatre and has been a guest lecturer
on the Wimbledon School of Art Theatre
Design MA. Rosa is also the Director of
Foundry18 which is part of the John Thaw
Initiative at The Actors Centre.

DAVID EDGAR

PLAYWRIGHT

RSC: Honorary Associate Artist. *Destiny*
(John Whiting award), *The Jail Diary
of Albie Sachs, Nicholas Nickleby*
**(Society of West End Theatres and
Tony awards),** *Maydays* **(Plays and
Players award),** *Dr Jekyll and Mr Hyde,
Pentecost* **(Evening Standard award),**
*The Prisoner's Dilemma, Written on the
Heart, Trying It On, A Christmas Carol.*
THIS SEASON: *Maydays, Trying It On.*
THEATRE INCLUDES: *Death Story, Mary
Barnes, Arthur & George* (Birmingham
Rep); *Wreckers* (7:84); *Our Own People*
(Pirate Jenny); *Teendreams* (with Susan
Todd, Monstrous Regiment); *Entertaining
Strangers* and *A Time to Keep* (with
Stephanie Dale, Dorchester Community
Play); *That Summer* (Hampstead Theatre);
*The Shape of the Table, Albert Speer,
Playing with Fire* (National Theatre);
Daughters of the Revolution and *Mothers
Against* (Oregon Shakespeare Festival/
Berkeley Rep); *Testing the Echo* (Out of

Joint); *Black Tulips* (part of The Great
Game/Tricycle); *If Only* (Chichester
Festival Theatre); *Trying it On* (Warwick
Arts Centre/tour).

TRANSLATIONS: *Galileo* (Birmingham
Rep); *The Master Builder* (Chichester
Festival Theatre); *Mother Courage*
(Shakespeare Festival, Stratford Ontario).

TELEVISION: Adaptations of stage plays
for television include *Baby Love, Destiny,
Nicholas Nickleby* and *The Jail Diary of
Albie Sachs.* Original television plays
include *Vote for Them* (with Neil Grant),
Buying a Landslide and *Citizen Locke*.

RADIO: Adaptations of stage plays include
*The Shape of the Table, Mary Barnes,
That Summer, Pentecost* and *Playing with
Fire*. Original work for radio includes
*Ecclesiastes, A Movie Starring Me, Talking
to Mars, The Secret Parts, Brave Faces*
and *Something Wrong about the Mouth.*

FILM: *Lady Jane.*

OTHER: *How Plays Work* (Nick Hern
Books). David Edgar founded Britain's
first MA in Playwriting Studies, at the
University of Birmingham in 1989.

CLAIRE GERRENS
LIGHTING DESIGNER
RSC: *#WeAreArrested, The Ant and the Cicada; Revolt. She said. Revolt again.* Claire joined the RSC Lighting Department in 2010.
THIS SEASON: *Maydays.*
TRAINED: Technical Theatre Arts, RADA.
THEATRE INCLUDES: In Claire's eight years at Stratford she has worked on a number of productions across the Courtyard, RST, Swan, TOP, UK and international tours and transfers, but her highlights so far include: Lighting Re-lighter and Programmer on *A Midsummer Night's Dream: A Play for the Nation*, Lighting Programmer on *The Tempest* (Stratford); Lighting Programmer on *Julius Caesar* (Stratford/UK and international tour); Lighting Re-lighter on *The Rape of Lucrece* (Stratford/UK, Ireland and international tour); Lighting Programmer on *Wendy & Peter Pan* (Stratford, 2013 and 2015).

KATE GODFREY
COMPANY VOICE AND TEXT WORK
RSC: Kate is Head of Voice, Text and Actors' Support. *Romeo and Juliet, Macbeth, Twelfth Night, Julius Caesar, Antony and Cleopatra, Titus Andronicus, Coriolanus, The Tempest, King Lear, Hamlet, Cymbeline, Henry V, King & Country Cycle.*
THIS SEASON: *Maydays.*
TRAINED: Central School of Speech and Drama.
THEATRE INCLUDES: Kate was a member of the voice faculty at the Guildhall School of Music and Drama for 20 years and an associate of the National Theatre's voice department since 2001. *One Man Two Guvnors, Dara, 3 Winters, Man and Superman, Three Days in the Country, The Red Lion, War Horse* and the Alan Bennett plays *People, The Habit of Art* and

The History Boys (National Theatre). She has worked on numerous productions in London's West End, and with rep companies such as Chichester Festival Theatre, Manchester Royal Exchange and Sheffield Crucible. She has also coached Japanese actors and directors in Kyoto and Osaka.
FILM INCLUDES: *Callas Forever, The December Boys, Victor Frankenstein* (with Daniel Radcliffe).

PIPPA HILL
DRAMATURG
RSC: *#WeAreArrested, Miss Littlewood, A Christmas Carol, The Earthworks, Vice Versa, The Hypocrite, The Seven Acts of Mercy, Fall of the Kingdom, Always Orange, Queen Anne, Don Quixote, Hecuba, Oppenheimer, The Christmas Truce, The Roaring Girl, The Ant and the Cicada, I Can Hear You, Wendy & Peter Pan, The Empress, The Thirteen Midnight Challenges of Angelus Diablo, Here Lies Mary Spindler.*
THIS SEASON: *Maydays.*
WORK INCLUDES: Pippa Hill is the Literary Manager at the RSC and oversees the commissioning and development of all the Company's new plays, adaptations and translations. She also works closely with the creative teams preparing the texts for the classical repertoire. She was previously the Literary Manager at Paines Plough running three nationwide writing initiatives designed to identify and develop new playwrights.

OWEN HORSLEY
DIRECTOR

RSC: As Director: *Salomé.* **As Associate Director:** *Henry V, Henry IV Parts I and II, Richard II* **(Stratford/UK tour/ Barbican, London/China/BAM, New York),** *Shakespeare Lives in 10 Downing Street, A Midsummer Night's Dream* **(RSC/Garsington Opera),** *FE The Famous Victories of Henry V* **(Stratford/ UK tour/Barbican, London).**
THIS SEASON: *Maydays.*
TRAINED: Drama Centre London.
THEATRE INCLUDES: In 2008 Owen formed Eyestrings Theatre Company with his production of Christopher Marlowe's *Edward II* at St Andrew's Crypt in Holborn. Further work with Eyestrings includes: *In Bed with Messalina* (Courtyard); *See What I See* (St Clement's Mental Hospital); *The Duchess of Malfi* (Southwark Playhouse/ UK tour). Owen is an Associate Director for Cheek by Jowl. He was Assistant Director to Declan Donnellan on *The Changeling* (2006), *Cymbeline* (2007), *Troilus and Cressida* (2008), *Macbeth* (2009-10) and *'Tis Pity She's a Whore* (2011), becoming Associate Director in 2010. Owen co-directed the 2013 tour of *'Tis Pity*. Other directing credits include *Outside on the Street* (Edinburgh Fringe/ Arcola); *Antony and Cleopatra, Lysistrata, As You Like It* (Guildhall School of Music and Drama); *Hungry Heart* (RADA). Owen also works extensively in Europe. He has led workshops in Spain, Italy, Luxembourg and France. His first Spanish production, *The Malcontent*, opened at the Almagro Festival in August 2011 before transferring to Madrid. In summer 2018 Owen directed Mozart's *Don Giovanni* at La Mama, New York.

SIMON WELLS
DESIGNER

RSC: *The Famous Victories of King Henry V* **(First Encounters);** *Shakespeare Lives in 10 Downing Street.*
THIS SEASON: *Maydays.*
TRAINED: Royal Central School of Speech and Drama (BA Hons Design for the Stage).
THEATRE INCLUDES: *The Sound of Music* (Costume Design. Opus Theatre, Sao Paulo); *Talking Heads* (Gala Theatre, Durham); *Promises Promises* (Southwark Playhouse); *Rapunzel* (Costume Design. Chickenshed Theatre); *Peter Pan, Children of the Night* (Oxford Playhouse); *Titanic The Musical, Like I Care, Applause* (ArtsEd, London); *A Twist of Lemmon* (St James Theatre, London); *Red Riding Hood* (Pleasance, London); *Cinderella and the Beanstalk* (Theatre503); *See What I Wanna See, The Dirty Talk, The Return of the Soldier* (Jermyn Street); *Bette Midler and Me* (Gatehouse Theatre/UK tour); *Clap Hands, The Cow Play* (Rosemary Branch, London).

I am very proud that the RSC is once again collaborating with David Edgar to bring his landmark play *Maydays* to a new audience. David has been courageous, diligent and generous in completely re-working his script and collaborating so inventively with director Owen Horsley and his creative team. They have completely and ingeniously re-imagined *Maydays* so that a new generation can discover its searching truths. This Mischief Festival continues our long-standing commitment to celebrating inspiring political writing at The Other Place which asks the hardest and most urgent questions about our world and its divisions. I look forward to welcoming you to this very special event.

Erica Whyman, Deputy Artistic Director, Autumn 2018

MAYDAYS & TRYING IT ON

David Edgar

Introduction

I was lucky enough to be born in 1948, and thus to be twenty (and in my second year at university) in 1968, the *annus mirabilis* of the worldwide student revolutionary Left. I'm not an autobiographical playwright, but the events and legacy of that momentous year have informed my writing ever since. In my 1983 play for the Royal Shakespeare Company, *Maydays*, I used my life story as the basis of a kind of counter-factual thought experiment about how that life might have turned out differently. Now, fifty years on from 1968, I've made a directly autobiographical solo show, in which I'm not only writing my life but playing it. At the same time, I've had the opportunity to revisit *Maydays* for a new production at the RSC.

Maydays arose out of my first play for the RSC, *Destiny*, which was a warning play about the rise of the neo-fascist National Front (a forerunner of the British National Party) in 1970s England. Turned down by theatres across the land (including my home theatre, the Birmingham Rep), the play was taken up by the RSC, and presented in its small Stratford studio theatre The Other Place (then a tin hut) in 1976, transferring to the company's large London theatre, the Aldwych, the following year. The play got many things right (predicting the rise of a pseudo-respectable tendency on the neo-fascist right in the 2000s) but its big mistake was underestimating how an enfeebled Conservative Party was being rejuvenated under its new leader Margaret Thatcher. By the time *Destiny* was televised in 1978, the National Front was in terminal decline, and the Conservatives were constructing a potent ideological cocktail of economic liberalism and social conservatism, the latter a backlash against the sexual permissiveness, youth counter-culture and hostility to traditional authority which defined the late 1960s. This cocktail attracted a winning coalition of traditional Conservatives, free-market libertarians and working-class voters to bring Mrs Thatcher to power in May 1979.

By then I was halfway through a year-long trip to the United States, where a similar coalition was being forged, between traditional Republicans, socially conservative religious voters (increasingly organised into campaigning groups like the Moral Majority) and, overlapping, a significant proportion of white working-class voters. But the alliance which was to take Ronald Reagan to victory in 1980 included another, much more surprising component, which couldn't be more different from the evangelical Christians of the Bible belt or the Redneck Republicans of the declining northern industrial states. This was a group of New York intellectuals, all of whom had been on the Left (some on the Communist or even Trotskyite Left) in their youths, but who had shifted dramatically to the right in middle age. Led by Irving Kristol (co-editor of the journal *The Public Interest*) these Neo-Conservatives defined themselves as 'liberals mugged by reality'. They were charily supportive of the free market (one of Kristol's essay compilations was titled *Two Cheers for Capitalism*) but defiantly hostile to the counter-culture of the 1960s. They provided a valuable intellectual endorsement to the Reagan campaign.

Returning to Thatcher's Britain, it was obvious that she – too – had relied on political defectors to bring her to power. As the death agony of the 1974–79 Labour government unfolded, former socialists and Communists rushed to contribute to proto-Thatcherite tirades with titles like *The Future that Doesn't Work* and *An Escape from George Orwell's 1984*. In 1978, former left-wingers such as Kingsley Amis, Max Beloff, Reg Prentice, Paul Johnson and Alun Chalfont anthologised their apostasy in a book proudly titled *Right Turn*. Their conviction that the late 1960s had unleashed a multi-headed demon of indiscipline was confirmed during the wave of strikes which broke over Britain in the chilly winter of 1978–9. As Tara Martin López points out in her book on *The Winter of Discontent*, many of the private- and public-sector strikers were black or female, had grown up in the late 1960s, and were inspired by the general rebelliousness of the time.

The Conservative response to these events was summed up graphically by Thatcher guru Alfred Sherman, who, as a young Communist, had fought for the Republican side in the Spanish

Civil War. 'As for the lumpen proletariat, coloured people and the Irish,' he declared, 'the only way to hold them in check is to have enough well-armed and properly trained police.' For Margaret Thatcher, who was to blame the urban riots of 1981 on the 'fashionable theories and permissive claptrap' of the 1960s, 'we would never have defeated socialism if it hadn't been for Sir Alfred'.

Thatcher and Reagan's defectors were by no means the first generation of radicals to leapfrog the centre ground and vault directly from the far-left to the die-hard right, a tendency satirised by critic Edmund Wilson in his satirical couplet about the formerly left-wing novelist John Dos Passos: 'On account of Soviet knavery / He favours restoring slavery.' For former radical beat critic and later neo-Conservative Norman Podhoretz, homosexuality was a death wish and feminism a plague.

The importance of defectors to the Conservative renewal of the 1980s led me to speculate about my own generation, radicalised not in the 1930s and 1940s, but in the era of Black Power, Women's Liberation and Vietnam. Certainly, there were examples of left–right movement, notably in France (the so-called *nouveaux philosophes*) and among some notable former radicals – black and white – in America. It was surely only a matter of time before a significant cohort of British *soixante-huitards* took the same journey. To write *Maydays*, I asked myself how someone like me would move rightwards. I used to quip – not entirely unseriously – that I wrote a play about a public-school-educated 1968 leftist moving to the Conservative right in order to stop that happening to me.

As the fiftieth anniversary of 1968 approached, I asked the RSC to think about reviving the play they'd premiered in the early 1980s. Increasingly, it was clear that the story of the play was growing ever more apposite. First, there were an increasing number of people from my generation heading right. Most notably, the brothers Christopher and Peter Hitchens became spokesmen for defection. Both had been members of the Trotskyite International Socialists; Peter jumped first, and is now a virulently social-conservative columnist on the *Daily Mail*. Christopher's desertion of the Left came to public prominence when he joined a number of formerly-Left belligerati in backing the 2003 invasion of Iraq, but his revealing 2010 memoir *Hitch-22* shows that he had sympathised with Margaret Thatcher since 1979 (supporting, among other things, the Falklands War).

Then, in the 2010s, there was an upsurge of youth protest, the most sustained and effective since the late 1960s, echoing the movements of the late 1960s in style and substance. From Wages for Housework to MeToo, from Black Power to Black Lives Matter, from Yippies levitating the Pentagon to UK Uncut invading Fortnum and Mason, the form and content of late sixties protest saw itself renewed nearly fifty years later. At the same time, the 2010s have seen the rise of a populist right which – like the Reagan and Thatcher movements – sought to unravel the gains of the 1960s, most dramatically in their opposition to mass immigration, but also in demands to roll back social and sexual reforms. While, behind both phenomena, there lay an underlying and growing political generation gap. In the 1960s, radicals counselled young activists not to trust anyone over thirty. At the 2017 General Election, the age at which a Labour majority turned into a Conservative one was forty-seven.

The RSC generously organised a couple of invaluable workshops on *Maydays*, during which two groups of actors explored how to turn what had been a contemporary play in the early 1980s into a history play for now (reminded that 1968 is as far away from 2018 as it is from 1918). This involved the creation of a chorus of contemporary actors, to guide a 2018 audience through the background history of post-war Britain, as well as pointing up contemporary resonances. The process gave me the opportunity to sharpen and deepen the personal stories of the characters. I also restructured the play's chronology, grouping together a series of scenes telling the story of a Soviet dissident, to point up the parallels and differences between Western and Eastern dissent. Finally, the chorus allowed us to reduce the massive 1983 Barbican Theatre cast to an Other-Place-manageable company of ten. The flexibility of The Other

Place studio theatre allowed designer Simon Wells to create not one setting environment but three. I owe a huge amount to director Owen Horsley for an inspiring and inventive production, and to dramaturg Pippa Hill for deftly guiding the play on its journey from 1983 to now.

Revisiting a play that started with my biography obviously begged the question of what's happened to me in the thirty-five years since *Maydays* was premiered. Happily, I had a unique opportunity to address it. Around the time I started talking to the RSC about *Maydays*, I was visiting the Warwick Arts Centre, and – over a drink in the bar – was asked by its director Alan Rivett about my plans. I blurted out that I'd always wanted to do a solo show and that, as the upcoming fiftieth anniversary of 1968 happened to be the seventieth anniversary of me, this might be a great time to fulfil that ambition. He asked me about its subject, I improvised the idea of a conversation between my seventy- and twenty-year-old selves, and he commissioned it on the spot.

The excellent China Plate theatre studio set up a process of workshopping and then making the show, the first with director Lu Kemp and the second with director Christopher Haydon. I am greatly indebted to them both. One of my first steps was to interview upwards of twenty-five people, most of them around my age, in order to ask two questions. One was why the generation liberated from the social and sexual restraints and narrow nationalism of the 1950s chose to vote substantially to turn its back on the open borders of the European Union. The second was what the veterans of 1968 had retained, in their political practice and their lives. Asking that question of them was, of course, a way of asking it of me. If *Maydays* posited a possible, negative answer, then *Trying It On* has the benefit of hindsight. I'm no longer a youthful revolutionary, but nor am I the crusty defector of proverbial age. In the argot of my youth, I hope I'm still hanging on in there.

David Edgar
September 2018

MAYDAYS

In memory of Jill Forbes

Characters

THE CHORUS

PART ONE:
England and America: 1945–1975

JEREMY CROWTHER
PAVEL LERMONTOV
MARTIN GLASS
JAMES GRAIN
PHIL
AMANDA
BRYONY
JUDY
PHYLLIS WEINER
POLICEMAN
DETECTIVE
PAPERSELLERS
TWO LIBERTARIANS
MRS GLASS
SMOKER
MOLLY

END OF PART ONE:
Glienicke Bridge: 1978

KGB OFFICER
AMBASSADOR
SVETLANA DANILOVA
MIKLOS PALOCZI

PART TWO:
The Eastern Bloc: 1956–1971

CLARA IVANOVNA
ERICA MOLNAR
OLD WOMAN
SOVIET SOLDIERS
SOVIET SERGEANT
YOUNG SOLDIER
HUNGARIAN PRISONERS
PUGACHEV
SKURATOV
GUARDS
KOROLENKO
PRISONER
OFFICER
DOCTOR
CHIEF OFFICER

PART THREE:
England: 1978–1984

REPORTERS
CAMERAMEN
OFFICIAL (HEATHROW)
SIR HUGH TRELAWNEY
WAITER
TANYA

Suggested Doubling

For a cast of ten:

JEREMY, PARTYGOER, SERGEANT, SKURATOV,
OFFICER

MARTIN, YOUNG SOLDIER

JAMES, PALOCZI

AMANDA, ERICA

CLARA, JUDY, 6TH PAPERSELLER, LIBERTARIAN,
SVETLANA

PHIL, 1ST PAPERSELLER, SMOKER, 1ST SOLDIER,
KOROLENKO, WAITER

BRYONY, 4TH PAPERSELLER, LIBERTARIAN, MOLLY,
2ND SOLDIER, TANYA

PHYLLIS WEINER, 3RD PAPERSELLER, MRS GLASS,
PARTYGOER, OLD WOMAN, KGB OFFICER, DOCTOR

LERMONTOV, 2ND PAPERSELLER

DETECTIVE, 5TH PAPERSELLER, PARTYGOER,
AMBASSADOR, PUGACHEV, CHIEF OFFICER,
TRELAWNEY

Languages

Although people speak in Russian and Hungarian, all languages
are rendered in English. When Lermontov is speaking English,
he does so with a Russian accent. Palozci speaks Russian well
enough not to need an accent; his English is good too, but
accented. When Lermontov and Palozci speak to each other,
without wishing others to hear, they speak in Russian, rendered
as accentless English.

On a couple of occasions, Lermontov asks Paloczi for an
English word. So, when he is groping for the word 'novelty',
we assume that the phrase 'new thing' is, as it were, the Russian
words for 'novelty'.

Notation

A forward slash (/) indicates when the next speaker begins
speaking.

May Days

5 May 1818	Karl Marx is born.
15 May 1848	A Communist rising in Paris is quickly overthrown.
28 May 1871	The Paris Commune falls after fifteen months in power.
1 May 1886	A Chicago strike for the eight-hour day leads to the founding of the international May Day workers' festival.
4 May 1919	The Bavarian Soviet is defeated after two weeks in power.
4 May 1926	The nine-day British General Strike begins.
3 May 1936	A left-wing popular front government is elected in France.
3 May 1937	Communists suppress anarchist revolutionaries in Barcelona.
2 May 1945	Berlin falls to the Red Army.
7 May 1954	The French are defeated by Communist Vietnamese forces at Dien Bien Phu.
10 May 1968	The Parisian 'Night of the Barricades' leads to a general strike by ten million workers.
1 May 1973	Two million British workers strike against anti-union legislation.
5 May 1982	Attempts to evict the women's peace camp at Greenham Common fail.

Part One

The thing that attracted me, even infatuated me, about the Communist movement was the feeling, however illusory, of being close to the helm of history... There was at the time, and with us youngsters in particular, an altogether idealist illusion that we were inaugurating a human era, an era where every man – every man – would be neither outside history nor under the heel of history, but would direct and create it himself...

Milan Kundera, *The Joke*, 1967

I allowed myself to be forced into the position of feeling guilty not only about my own indecisions, but about the very virtues of love and pity and a passion for personal freedom which had brought me close to Communism. The Communists told me that these feelings were 'bourgeois'. The Communist, having joined the Party, has to castrate himself of the reasons which made him one.

Stephen Spender, *The God that Failed*, 1950

We shall not enter the kingdom of socialism in white gloves on a polished floor.

Leon Trotsky, December 1917

Scene One

May Day 1945. England. Enter a young man, JEREMY
CROWTHER, *from the Midlands. He has a soapbox and a red
flag. He climbs on the soapbox.*

The CHORUS *consists of actors in the present day.*

CHORUS. May Day.

　The traditional spring festival.

　The universal distress call.

　The International Workers' Day.

　Leicester, 1945.

JEREMY. Friends. This May Day of all May Days we celebrate
　the achievements of the international working class.

CHORUS. Jeremy.

　Seventeen.

JEREMY. Fascism has been defeated! The war is won!

CHORUS. The next day, the victorious Soviet Army will raise
　the Red Flag over the Reichstag in Berlin.

JEREMY. At last we face a future of peace and progress!

CHORUS. Three months later, the Labour Party will win a
　landslide victory in the British General Election.

JEREMY. An end to colonialism!

CHORUS. Two years later, India will win independence from
　Britain.

JEREMY. No return to the poverty and misery of the 1930s!

CHORUS. In 1948, the British National Health Service will be
　created.

The Welfare State.

An end to squalor,

ignorance,

idleness,

disease,

and want.

JEREMY. We Communists have been asked a thousand times what we mean by socialism. We answer: look at the heroic achievements of the Soviet state and people. As throughout the world the toiling masses rise to liberate themselves from tyranny, we can at last say: *this* is what we meant.

JEREMY *gets down from his soapbox.*

CHORUS. But by 1949, both the Americans and Soviets will possess the atom bomb, and the Cold War has begun.

The nuclear arms race.

Balance of terror.

In the early 1950s, ruling Communist parties in eastern Europe...

Czechoslovakia,

East Germany,

Poland,

Hungary...

...will establish a Soviet-style apparatus of secret police, show trials, purges and labour camps.

On 4 November 1956, the Soviet Union will invade Hungary, to suppress a democratic uprising against the Communist regime.

We see a Soviet army officer, who we will later meet as PAVEL LERMONTOV. *Enter* MARTIN GLASS, *a schoolboy in Cadet Force uniform. He marches round the stage. We see he is wearing the badge of the Campaign for Nuclear Disarmament.*

Two years later, the British Campaign for Nuclear Disarmament will be founded.

And, in November 1962, the crisis over Soviet nuclear missiles in Communist Cuba will threaten nuclear catastrophe.

1962.

The parade ground of a minor public school in Wiltshire.

Martin.

Seventeen.

MARTIN *stops and stands still.*

Scene Two

Spring, 1962. The parade ground of a minor public school. It is pouring with rain. MARTIN is dripping wet. He's been out here for some considerable time.

A schoolmaster cycles on to the stage. It's JEREMY, now thirty-three, wearing a black plastic mac and a black Sou'wester. He cycles to MARTIN, stops, and dismounts. MARTIN comes to attention.

JEREMY. Uh – Glass, isn't it?

MARTIN. Glass, Martin B, yes, sir.

   Slight pause.

JEREMY. It's – pretty wet out here, Glass.

MARTIN. Yes, it is that, sir.

   Slight pause.

JEREMY. Now, you're in St Augustine, am I right?

MARTIN. No, sir. Sir Thomas More.

JEREMY. I see.

> *Slight pause.*

> Well, um, whatever, shouldn't you be there? I mean, parade fell out, what, best part of two hours ago.

> *Slight pause.*

> Glass, what are you doing here?

MARTIN. I was ordered to stay here, sir. After fall-out, sir. By Mr Sands. The adjutant.

JEREMY. Yes. Why?

MARTIN. Gross disrespect for the Queen's uniform, sir.

> JEREMY *is forced to acknowledge* MARTIN*'s badge.*

JEREMY. Oh, yes. Of course. Did Mr Sands give any indication of how long...

MARTIN. Till further notice, sir.

JEREMY. I see.

> *Pause.* JEREMY *looks up to the sky.*

> You know, the badge, it's interesting... The shape, I mean the actual construction of the symbol...

MARTIN. Is it, sir?

JEREMY. Yes. It's very clever, the, uh, two arms at the bottom, are the semaphore for N, nuclear, the top bit is the semaphore for D, disarmament, the middle as a whole's the broken cross, symbolic of the death of man, while the circle, you see, represents the unborn child... Look, this is madness, you'll catch your death, I think you must come in.

MARTIN. Is that an order, sir?

JEREMY. Well, if you like.

MARTIN. It's not really a question of what I like.

JEREMY. All right, then. It's an order.

MARTIN (*to attention*). Sir!

Then MARTIN *breaks attention and makes to go.*

JEREMY. Look, Glass… Sir Thomas More is miles away. My cottage is just over there. I think you ought to get something hot to drink.

MARTIN *turns back to him*

MARTIN. Yes, sir. Fucking right.

MARTIN leaves. JEREMY comes downstage and starts to take off his waterproofs, as a table and three chairs – on one of which hangs the jacket of MARTIN*'s sodden uniform – are set up.* JEREMY *calls offstage.*

JEREMY. So what did he say then?

MARTIN (*offstage*). Who, sir?

JEREMY. Mr Sands.

MARTIN (*offstage*). Well, in summary: Loyalty to Queen and Country. Better dead than Red. Send all the darkies home. And if you don't agree with that it's because your people are too la-di-dah.

Enter MARTIN, *rubbing his hair with a towel.*

JEREMY. And are they?

MARTIN. My pa's a vicar. They can hardly pay the fees.

JEREMY. Do you want some Horlicks?

MARTIN. You bet. Thanks.

He sits and sips a mug of Horlicks at the table.

JEREMY. Why do they keep you here, then?

MARTIN. Oh, I think… some sad, pathetic concept of propriety. My mother's concept, that is. Military stock. She's a very proper woman.

JEREMY *laughs*.

I mean, like the vicarage is next door to a US Air Force base,
bang in the fucking firing line, so she supports the
annihilation of the species as a simple point of social
etiquette. You know.

JEREMY *laughs again*.

I mean they've got a 1957 Morris Oxford. And when they
come to Speech Day, she insists they park it half a mile away
and walk. So as not to Show Me Up. As if I cared.

JEREMY. You sound as if you care.

MARTIN. Well, it makes me angry. As if it mattered, where I
came from.

JEREMY (*with a gesture to the badge on* MARTIN's *tunic*).
And that? That makes you angry too?

MARTIN. Not in the same way, no, sir. That is because it's
right. As I imagine you think too.

JEREMY. Well, as it happens, I have sat down in my time.

During this speech, MARTIN *takes out ten cigarettes, and a
box of matches. He takes out a cigarette and opens the
matches. They are sodden.*

MARTIN. Then I imagine you'd resent as much as I do the idea
you only want to ban the bomb because of who your people
are. That you don't think what you think, and you don't feel
what you feel.

JEREMY *is looking on in some panic*.

Look, sir. I'm sorry, but it has been quite a day. Do you have
a light?

JEREMY. A light?

MARTIN *rattles the damp matches*.

Look, Glass, strictly speaking...

As he finds a box of matches and gives them to MARTIN,
lamely:

They're terribly bad for you.

MARTIN (*lighting up*). I'm always keen to see, sir, how far people are prepared to go.

JEREMY. Well, are you now.

MARTIN. And in your case, sir, it's particularly interesting to me, how you end up teaching here at all.

JEREMY. Why's that?

MARTIN. Being a Communist, and so on.

Pause.

JEREMY. Um, what makes you –

MARTIN. Wavish, Roger P, in Sir Isaac Newton, has this pa who was a Red at Trinity. Trinity, Cambridge? And for a birthday present, he gave me a copy of the *Daily Worker* for the day that I was born. May the second, 1945.

Slight pause.

I assume that you're the same JH Crowther, sir? Speaking to an enthusiastic crowd in Leicester? 'Throughout the world, the toiling masses rise'?

JEREMY. Well…

MARTIN. I mean, a ban-the-bomber, you could just be a Methodist or a nudist or a vegetarian. But actually a Communist. Actually in The Party. Wavish and I view that as really cool.

Pause.

JEREMY. Well, I'm afraid I'm not in it any more.

MARTIN. Why not, sir?

JEREMY. Because I left it over Hungary. Hungary?

MARTIN. The Soviet Invasion. 1956. Suppressing democratic reform.

JEREMY. Which the Party decided it approved of. The invasion, that is. Not the reform.

MARTIN. Why?

Slight pause.

JEREMY. All right. They sent this apparatchik up from London,
to explain the Party line. Accusing those brave, wild
revolutionaries in the streets of Budapest of being –
'objectively' – the agents of American imperialism. And I'd
joined the Party to liberate the oppressed, and here it was,
telling me I have to back people doing the oppressing. And I
thought – oh, come on, do you really want this man to run
the country? And I left.

MARTIN. But surely, sir, you're still a socialist.

JEREMY. Well, I / suppose –

MARTIN. I mean, you haven't left the *Left*.

JEREMY. Look. I'm not Wavish Senior. I wasn't a Red at Trinity.
In fact, I was born in Mansfield. And I went to grammar school
and I had a lady teacher whose husband had died fighting for
the Republicans in Spain.When I was nine. And the reason why
he'd gone was his unshakable belief that once the world was
liberated from the shackles of the capitalist system, every
worker could become an Aristotle or a Michelangelo.

MARTIN. Well, crumbs.

JEREMY. And then, when I was seventeen –

MARTIN *acknowledges.*

– we won the war and got our Labour government. Which
set about to free the masses from the poverty and misery
which I'd seen around me in the thirties. And indeed the
workers got their national assistance and their council houses
and the National Health Service, but also unthinkable
material prosperity. All those television sets and Hoover
Automatics, even Mini Coopers…

MARTIN. But?

JEREMY. But I have to say, I wondered – I still wonder – if all
that was really what we meant, at all?

A glance at his watch:

Now, look, Glass, it's nearly curfew –

MARTIN. You mean, as opposed to, every brickie being Aristotle.

JEREMY. Well, perhaps that was a silly way of putting it...

MARTIN. Oh, do you think so, sir?

MARTIN *takes off the dressing gown and puts on the jacket of his uniform.*

Because it seems to me, sir, there's a danger, you can see the mass of people just as victims. Of the poverty and misery. Passive and inert. But just because the Labour Party hasn't built the New Jerusalem, and the Communists have let the revolution down – let you down – does that mean we have to give up on the whole idea?

JEREMY. Well, of course, I haven't –

MARTIN. Because, mightn't there be other ways of building socialism, and other people who might build it? Young people? Black people? People who we haven't thought of? And if those people really cracked the shackles of the system for themselves – who knows how many Michelangelos could bloom?

I'm sorry, sir.

JEREMY. No, no.

MARTIN. But I'm with you. I'm with the brave wild revolutionaries in Hungary. And I'm sure, if I was you, I'd want to be a Red – at Trinity or anywhere – who'd been to Spain.

He looks at his watch. He should be back at his house.

Thanks for the Horlicks, sir. Goodnight.

He goes. JEREMY*, alone, picks up the Horlicks mug.*

JEREMY. Glass. Go to America.

He picks up the ashtray.

Scene Three

MARTIN *changes from a schoolboy to a backpacker, travelling across America, in the summer of 1967.*

CHORUS. 1962. Bob Dylan records 'Blowin' in the Wind'.

MARTIN. And fifty-nine young Americans met in Port Huron, Michigan, to draw up a manifesto for a body called Students for a Democratic Society. It asserted that 'men are infinitely precious, and possessed of unfulfilled capacities for reason, freedom and love'. A New Left, freed from loyalty to the USSR, dedicated to the liberation of all humankind from exploitation and oppression. Starting now.

CHORUS. August 1963: Martin Luther King delivers his 'I have a dream' speech in Washington.

MARTIN. I've seen young men and women, some the children of former Communists, many Jewish, marching, riding, fighting and sometimes dying alongside negro activists, to desegregate the south.

CHORUS. A year later. Three civil rights workers are murdered in Mississippi.

And civil rights marchers are attacked by police on a bridge in Selma, Alabama.

MARTIN. I've met students: insisting on their right to campaign for civil rights, on campus. Working to organise the black and white poor in the northern cities. Fighting the drafting of students into the army. Stopping the war machine, by any means necessary.

CHORUS. In 1966, the Americans drafted three hundred and eighty-two thousand young men into the military, to fight the so-called Viet Cong in Vietnam.

But. 1967: The Summer of Love in San Francisco.

Flower power.

MARTIN. But. Draft-card burning. Blocking troop trains.

CHORUS. 'Hell no, we won't go.'

Draft evader: Muhammad Ali.

Draft evader: Donald Trump.

MARTIN. Seeing the future of the revolution with the marginalised and the excluded. The colonised peoples in the US and beyond its borders. The liberation armies of the third world and the first. The children of the enemy, prefiguring the New Jerusalem. Breaking down the gates, from Saigon to Washington. Bringing down a President.

Audio or footage:

LYNDON JOHNSON. I shall not seek, and will not accept, the nomination of my party for another term as your president.

MARTIN. Becoming a new person. Never going home.

Scene Four

A meeting hall in a students union in the Midlands, May 1968.
JAMES GRAIN *is thirty-five.*

JAMES. Comrades, my name is Grain, and I'm on the Central Committee of an organisation called Socialist Vanguard.

CHORUS. May 1968.

Somewhere in the Midlands.

England.

JAMES. Comrades, this is an extraordinary meeting, and it is a measure of the extraordinary epoch through which we are moving. As countless speakers have stated here today, we have witnessed, over the last five months, events that would have seemed unthinkable even a year ago. In the new year, a guerrilla peasant army fights its way into the US Embassy in the capital of South Vietnam. As a result, in March: the de facto resignation of the President of the United States. April: the assassination of Martin Luther King provokes uprisings across America. And now, today, in France, not just protesting students but striking workers pose a challenge, not only to this government or that, but to the power and legitimacy of the state itself. And we can see it even here.

But, comrades, forgive me for one note of caution. Comrades, read the writing on the wall.

He gestures to the banners that we imagine are hung around the hall.

'Don't demand: occupy.' Yes, that's fine. 'Be realistic: demand the impossible.' Well, if you like. 'Victory to the Viet Cong.' That's good too, we don't want peace in Vietnam, but American defeat.

'The Revolution is the Festival of the Oppressed.' That's very good indeed. But in fact, it's only half the story.

It's a quote from Lenin. Yes, I'm afraid so, Lenin. Let me read the whole of it to you.

(*Reads:*) 'Revolutions are festivals of the oppressed and exploited... At such times the people are capable of performing miracles. But we shall be traitors and betrayers of the revolution, if we do not use the festive energy of the masses to wage a ruthless and self-sacrificing struggle for the direct and decisive path...'

What is that path? Where should we go? What Is To Be Done?

Pause. He looks round.

Let me explain.

Scene Five

An old house in the Midlands, May 1968. Mid-evening. A
sitting-room area, with old furniture, a black-and-white TV set,
sleeping bags. Downstage is the eating part of the kitchen: a
table, chairs, a plastic clothes basket. On a washing line, some
nappies and three used inky stencils, their backing sheets on the
back, hung up with clothes pegs to dry.

PHIL *is running off a leaflet on an old Roneo duplicator. He's*
twenty, from Birmingham. The duplicator run finishes. He
removes the inky stencil, attaches the backing sheet, takes a
nappy down, tosses it in the clothes basket, and hangs up the
stencil on the line. As he puts another stencil on to the machine,
AMANDA *enters from another part of the house, with a tray of*
dirty mugs. She is twenty-one.

PHIL *tries to restart the duplicator. It doesn't go.*

PHIL. Oh, come on. Just for Mother, eh?

He kicks the machine. It starts.

I love you.

AMANDA. I don't believe this.

PHIL. So then, what d'you think?

AMANDA. Of what?

PHIL. The Roneo. I got it, knock-down, from the Catholic
    Association. I wasn't sure they'd take to selling off their
    surplus to the Socialist Society, so I told 'em I was from the
    Hockey Club. Apparently, they need the cash for a trip to
    Lourdes.

The machine stops.

They could have taken this along as well.

He hits the machine. It goes.

Ave Maria.

Enter MARTIN *from the street.*

AMANDA. Martin.

MARTIN. Amanda.

AMANDA. How was the conference?

MARTIN. Weren't you there?

AMANDA. Of course I wasn't there. I was dragging Tanya all round fucking Lipton's, wasn't I?

MARTIN. Par for the course. Maoists all morning, Trots all afternoon.

AMANDA. Which Trots?

MARTIN. Socialist Vanguard.

PHIL *is changing the stencil.*

AMANDA. Take care, sir. You speak of the Party I love.

MARTIN. I know.

AMANDA. Now, where are the Leeds Two, I wonder?

Doorbell.

Ah. They've lost another key.

She goes to answer the door.

PHIL. Hey, mate. Don't tell me, you're tempted.

MARTIN. What by?

PHIL. The wicked Trots.

MARTIN. Why shouldn't I be tempted?

PHIL. Cos I'll tell you what they'll say. 'Oh, we're not like the Commies. We don't do labour camps or purges. Our hero's Trotsky, for fuck's sake, and Stalin did him in.' But come down to it, like Trotsky, they're all for the Party Line. Ends justifying means. 'Revolutionary Discipline.' Deep down, it's power. Just The Same.

MARTIN (*helping* PHIL *with his duplicating*). Well, my basic
    problem with the Socialist Vanguard is more prosaic. It's
    that, if you want to be a member, they tell you the ten
    funniest jokes in the history of the world –

PHIL. And if you don't smile once –

PHIL *and* MARTIN. You're in.

    AMANDA *has brought in* JAMES.

JAMES. Good evening. I'm James Grain.

MARTIN. Oh, yes. Hallo.

JAMES. And I assure you, I'm a laugh a minute.

AMANDA. Sit down, James.

JAMES. Thank you.

    JAMES *sits at the table*. PHIL *returns to his work. A bang at
    the door. Enter* BRYONY *and* JUDY. *They are students
    from Leeds*.

BRYONY. Hi, Mand.

JUDY. Hi, Mand.

AMANDA. Hi, Bry. Hi, Jude.

JUDY. Hi, Mart.

MARTIN. Hi, Jude. Hi, Bry.

BRYONY. Hi, Phil.

PHIL. Hi, Bry.

JUDY. Hey, news.

BRYONY. Yur, right. Hi, Mart.

PHIL. Hi, hi.

    BRYONY *puts on the television*.

JAMES. I'm finding this a bit hard to work out.

    We see the flicker of the television on the faces of BRYONY
    and JUDY, *who are watching the* Nine O'Clock News.

AMANDA. Bryony and Judy are from Leeds, for the conference. Martin is my permanent lodger. Phil is crashing.

PHIL, *a smiley look; he's been crashing for some time.*

JAMES (*'Which?'*). Martin?

AMANDA (*indicating*). Allegedly studying for an MA on the anti-war movement in America.

MARTIN. Actually studying for an MA on the / anti-war –

JAMES. Yes, I read his pieces in – what was it? *Insurrection*?

MARTIN. *Stick Up.*

JAMES. 'Sieze the Time: from Resistance to Revolution.'

MARTIN (*impressed*). Yes.

AMANDA (*to* JAMES). So. Tell him.

MARTIN. Tell me what?

JAMES. That it might be time you joined.

MARTIN. Joined what?

JAMES. A revolutionary party.

MARTIN. Do you have one in mind?

JAMES. Socialist Vanguard is a revolutionary grouping of militant youths, students, intellectuals and above all, / workers.

PHIL (*mouthing, to* MARTIN). Workers.

JAMES. We are not to be confused with the Socialist Alliance, from whom we split, or the Left Opposition, who split from us, or Workers' Struggle, who split from them, or with the League for Revolutionary Socialism, who never split at all, they just burn people out, hence the 'ten funniest jokes' joke, which was first used about them when you were still in nappies. All clear so far?

MARTIN. Yes. Absolutely. What's the difference?

JAMES. They're wrong and we're right.

MARTIN. Right about what?

JAMES. Well, where to start?

Slight pause.

I'd say – primarily – we're right in being internationalists. In ascribing the failure of the Soviet Revolution to Stalin's attempt to build / socialism in one country.

PHIL (*mouthing, to* MARTIN). Socialism in one country.

MARTIN. Not the purges and the show trials and the labour camps.

AMANDA. Of course the show trials and / the camps.

JAMES. But we are also right to put no faith in this or any other Labour government, and their doomed pursuit of the / parliamentary road to socialism.

PHIL (*mouthing, to* MARTIN). Parliamentary road to socialism.

MARTIN. And their craven support for the Americans in / Vietnam.

JAMES. And we're right too to believe that the world-wide uprising of young people against that war in Vietnam – what you describe so elegantly in your articles about America – is in some ways a genuinely / revolutionary phenomenon.

PHIL (*mouthing, to* MARTIN). Genuinely revolutionary phenomenon.

Irked beyond measure, PHIL *goes to watch the news.*

MARTIN. Well, I couldn't put it better my –

JAMES. Believing that you can build the New Jerusalem within the very belly of the monster, in the here and now. Insisting, if you aren't prepared to live the revolution, every day, then the revolution that you make will unmake you.

MARTIN. I think, in fact, that is how I put it. Glad that you agree.

JAMES. I think, in fact, about your articles, the word I used was 'elegant'.

Pause.

MARTIN. Go on.

JAMES. Because our fundamental difference with you is that we see the essential agent of the revolution not as students or hippies but as the working class of the capitalist West. Just as Marx and Lenin said.

MARTIN. Well, as I understand it, the agent of the current uprising in Paris / is –

JAMES. The students. Absolutely. The children of the enemy.

MARTIN. And, in fact, it all kicked off / with –

JAMES. With protests over male and female students' dormitory arrangements, at –

MARTIN/JAMES. – the University of Paris at Nanterre.

JAMES. But if you're serious about a revolution, then it can't end there. Which is why we're in the business of turning anarchists and hippies into revolutionary socialists, and not the other way round.

MARTIN. You mean, turn –

He makes the peace sign – Churchill's Victory-V.

– to –

He makes the clenched-fist sign.

JAMES. Well, if you like.

MARTIN. Not sure I do.

JAMES. Then do ask yourself the question, if we don't, where your hippies will be in five years' time, when the festival is over, and it's back to the long haul? Where will you be?

MARTIN. I'm sorry, I don't understand.

PHIL *returning.*

JAMES. They will find that in the long term it just doesn't work. That you can't build islands of pure socialism in the capitalist sea. And they'll either drift back to the politics of their parents, or they'll take revenge upon the inadequacies of the world by turning to the bullet and the bomb, the weapons of despair.

So it is legitimate to ask of them, of you: what sacrifices are you prepared to make, to prove that you're committed to all this, that you're a real traitor to your class, that you're not just – on holiday?

MARTIN. You think that I'm / on holiday?

PHIL. Um, I don't like to interrupt –

AMANDA. What, Phil?

PHIL. But there's all these revolutionary students on the streets of Paris...

JAMES *moves quickly to the television.*

JAMES. How many?

JUDY. They say a million.

PHIL. Protesting against police brutality.

JAMES. And the general strike?

JUDY. Holding.

BRYONY. Spreading.

PHIL. Occupying factories.

JAMES. Right. Look. For twenty years or so, the myth's been growing that the working class has been bought off by – how did you put it? – television sets and Hoover Automatics. But do you know what's happening? Catastrophe. The workers haven't heard they've been bought off. Someone forgot to tell them, obviously, and millions of them are out on strike in France today.

Which is why, although we have no truck with labour camps and purges...

PHIL (*to* MARTIN). Aha!

JAMES. We do believe in the need for revolutionary discipline.

PHIL. Oho.

JAMES. To protect ourselves from the very forces of the state which have been unleashed on the students and the workers on the streets of France. To aspire to lead those workers towards the seizure of state power. And thereby to change human history.

PHIL *waves his arms in mock-despair and returns to his duplicator.*

MARTIN (*suddenly, to* AMANDA). Do you agree with this?

AMANDA. Martin. It would be wonderful if it could all be nice. 'Make love not war.' CND marchers, singing 'We Shall Overcome', as they shuffle through a dripping English Easter afternoon.

MARTIN. What, to protect the planet from destruction. Kind of like, to save the world.

AMANDA. But there comes a point when you have to think about the people on the other side.

MARTIN. What other side?

AMANDA. Like, my father-in-law is in the building trade. Employs three men. And treats them better than he treats himself. How can it possibly be moral, right or good, to take that firm away from him? But the point that that little firm is just the bottom of a pyramid. And at the top sit General Motors, Boeing, Standard Oil, and Bank of America. And he understands that if they go, he goes. And there are millions like him. Little people, owning their own houses, with privet hedges, carriage clocks and Morris Minors and maybe a bit of private income which they can't afford to lose. The kind of people who supported Hitler in Germany, not because they liked him, but because for them the alternative was losing everything. And who come the crunch will take up arms, will fight and kill, to keep that pyramid in place.

JAMES. Yes, there is that phrase of Trotsky's.

MARTIN. Oh, what's that?

JAMES. 'Human dust.'

Pause.

PHIL. Deep down. Just the same.

Pause.

MARTIN. Yes.

He turns to BRYONY, JUDY *and* PHIL.

Now, look, it's half-nine, does anybody fancy one before they close?

BRYONY. Why not.

JUDY. Sure thing.

PHIL. Let's go.

BRYONY, JUDY *and* PHIL *go out.*

MARTIN. 'Human dust.' Goodnight.

MARTIN *goes.* JAMES *and* AMANDA *left alone.*

AMANDA. Well, I guess, it's only rock'n'roll.

JAMES. I must go too.

AMANDA. Oh, must you?

JAMES. Catch the last train. We've an emergency political committee, early in the morning.

AMANDA. Well, of course. Unless…

Pause.

I've got some Scotch, I think, in case you'd like one for the road.

JAMES. Well, that might be very nice.

AMANDA *finds half a bottle of Scotch and two glasses. She pours.*

AMANDA. And in fact… In fact, there is a train at seven-thirty in the morning. Gets you into London, oh, by nine-fifteen.

Slight pause.

If you should care to…

JAMES. Well, that might be even nicer.

AMANDA *gives* JAMES *his Scotch.*

Father-in-law?

AMANDA. We separated. Shortly after Tanya –

JAMES. Yes.

Pause.

AMANDA. It *might* be nicer?

JAMES *smiles.* AMANDA *takes his hand to lead him out when* MARTIN *bursts back in.*

MARTIN. Look –

AMANDA *and* JAMES *stop.*

Look, the point is, that I didn't mean…

He clocks some of the situation.

But I have decided. No.

Slight pause.

JAMES. Well, history will have to muddle on without you, Martin.

MARTIN *goes.* AMANDA *turns to the audience.*

AMANDA. By the end of May, ten million workers will be out on strike in France.

JAMES. But, June: President de Gaulle will win a landslide victory in a general election.

AMANDA. August: Anti-war protests at the Democratic Party Convention will be brutally attacked by the Chicago police.

JAMES. November: Richard Nixon will be elected President of the United States.

AMANDA. And the twenty-year-old Vietnam war goes on.

Scene Six

A corridor in a building in Leeds University. Towards the end of 1969. Off the corridor, an office with a desk. On it, a telephone, a Dictaphone, and a certain amount of mess, paper cups, beer cans, etc. In actuality or imagination, slogans sprayed on the wall.

Meanwhile, in what we will learn is a nearby building, an American professor, PHYLLIS WEINER, *is speaking to a meeting. During this,* JEREMY *will come into the corridor. He wears an overcoat, and carries a briefcase. A knot of* STUDENTS, *a little way away, in animated discussion.*

WEINER. Okay. 1946. The Communists begin their guerrilla war in Vietnam.

　　1954. Trained by the Chinese, the Vietnamese Communists take over the north of that country.

　　The north finances and directs an insurgency by the Communist Viet Cong against the south.

HECKLER. Long live Ho Chi Minh!

WEINER. By 1965 we've sent in two hundred thousand young Americans to protect it.

HECKLER. Warmongers! US out!

WEINER. 1968. The Viet Cong new-year offensive kills thousands of civilians.

HECKLER. Victory to the Viet Cong!

WEINER. And in 1969, an American professor is invited to join a panel on these matters at a British university, which is occupied by protesting students, and the panel has to be conducted in a sports hall under police guard.

JEREMY *is looking at the slogans.*

CHORUS. No warmongers on campus.

The University of Life.

WEINER *and the* HECKLERS *have gone.*

JEREMY. Sadly, in fact, the University of Leeds.

JEREMY *turns to go into the office. One of the students notices* JEREMY. *It's* JUDY.

JUDY. What the hell...

Coming over to JEREMY.

Excuse me, 'scuse me –

JEREMY. Yes?

JUDY. Who are you?

JEREMY. My name is Crowther. I teach English Studies. This is my office. Who are you?

JUDY. How did you get in here?

JEREMY. I walked in.

JUDY. Through the lobby?

JEREMY. No, the mezzanine. It's easier, from where I park my car. Why d'you ask?

JUDY (*calls to the other students*). The mezzanine!

A couple of STUDENTS *rush out.* BRYONY *comes over to* JEREMY *and* JUDY.

JUDY. I'm sorry, but you shouldn't have got in. The building's occupied.

JEREMY. I see. By whom?

JUDY. By us.

JEREMY. Who's us?

JUDY. The students' union.

JEREMY. I thought you had a building of your own.

Very slight pause.

I'm sorry, what I mean is –

BRYONY. Hi. The reason for this occupation is that the university is is allowing imperialist warmongers to speak on campus. Please – do have a leaflet.

JEREMY. Thank you.

BRYONY. You're welcome.

JEREMY. Well, now, look, I'm sure it's most objectionable –

JEREMY *looking at the leaflet, as he speaks.*

BRYONY. Then why don't you object?

JEREMY. But I've got a class to give –

JUDY. Oh, go on, teacher. Be a traitor to your class.

JEREMY (*snaps*). Are you aware… that, in this document, you have, at a cursory glance, split two infinitives?

JUDY *and* BRYONY *look at each other.*

And that the person whose free speech you are currently suppressing, Phyllis – two Ls – Weiner, is a distinguished Professor of International Relations at the University of Georgetown?

BRYONY. A distinguished warmonger.

JEREMY. And are you, I just ask for information, actually serious in claiming that this – seat of learning is 'a velvet glove, wrapped round the fist of neo-fascism'?

Slight pause.

That's F–A–S–H–I–S–M?

BRYONY. Look, it's very simple.

JUDY. Military propaganda –

JEREMY (*moving to the door at his office*). Yes, I fully understand the *casus belli*, but I must insist –

JUDY (*blocking* JEREMY). Beg pardon. *Casus*-what?

JUDY *and* JEREMY *glare at each other.*

JEREMY. It's an expression, taken from the Latin. Latin is a language, spoken many years ago in Italy, / by –

JUDY. My dad was in the war. Conscripted, from a back-to-back in Huddersfield. He didn't see an inside tap till he was seventeen. At nineteen half his face was blown away, on a beach in Normandy called Gold. You take one step, I'll kick your balls in, sir.

Pause.

JEREMY. I fought for this. I fought for you. Wrote books and articles. Gave evidence to commissions. To cut a clearing in the groves of academe, for People Just Like You.

JUDY. Well, thanks a fucking bunch.

She turns to go. AMANDA *comes in.*

AMANDA. Okay. They've sent the pigs in. Swarming through the lobby.

BRYONY. Let's go.

AMANDA. And the mezzanine.

JUDY *gestures that she and* BRYONY *should go to the two locations. They kiss and* BRYONY *heads off.* AMANDA *hadn't known this. She smiles.* JEREMY *looks surprised.* AMANDA *looks at* JEREMY.

JEREMY. I am – if you'd just listen – on your bloody side.

AMANDA (*to* JUDY, *re:* JEREMY). Who's this?

JUDY. It's nobody.

JUDY *goes out, in the opposite direction to* BRYONY.

AMANDA (*to* JEREMY). It's only rock'n'roll.

> AMANDA *goes out too.* JEREMY *realises he's alone. He takes out his keys, goes to the office. Realises the door is ajar. Pushes it open. He goes in. Drinks in the scene. He sits and picks up the phone.*

JEREMY. Hallo? The revolution is the festival of what?

> *He puts the phone down. Then, in a sudden gesture, he sweeps the paper cups and debris off the desk. He takes a document from his briefcase and looks at it.* LERMONTOV *stands, without a tie, as if at a trial.* JEREMY *takes a Dictaphone from a drawer and starts to dictate:*

Letter to *The Times*. Dear Sir, I would like to bring to your attention... the case of PM Lermontov, that's P for – puerile, M for mayhem, L–E–R–M–O–N–T–O–V, a translator in a Moscow research institute, who has recently been sentenced to five years in a labour camp, for circulating a petition in support of protests against the Soviet invasion of Czech, that's C–Z–E–C–H–*O* – for outrage – slovakia.

> *Two* POLICEMEN *run on, ending up at* JEREMY*'s room.*

In view of the hostility currently displayed by British students protestors – in inverted commas – to dissident opinion –

> *The* POLICEMEN *enter* JEREMY*'s room..*

POLICEMAN. Ah, professor. Have you seen – ?

JEREMY (*pointing after* AMANDA *and* JUDY). Thataway.

Scene Seven

AMANDA*'s house. The* CHORUS.

CHORUS. Late 1969. In Britain, anti-Apartheid protestors
   mount a campaign of distruption to stop the upcoming all-
   white South African cricket tour.

   30 April 1970. President Nixon announces the US invasion
   of Cambodia.

   As she hangs her toddler daughter's clothes on the line,
   AMANDA *watches* PRESIDENT NIXON*'s broadcast.*

NIXON. This is not an invasion of Cambodia.

AMANDA. May Day. First May Day of the new decade. And
   the President of the United States goes mad.

   Door slam. AMANDA *turns off the radio. Enter* MARTIN
   and PHIL. MARTIN *is in vaguely paramilitary gear,
   including bits of his old army uniform.* PHIL *wears a
   headband, which is bloody.* MARTIN *is mildly injured – cuts
   and bruises.* PHIL *is bleeding a lot.*

MARTIN *(heavily sarcastic).* Well, have we not had the very
   merriest of May Days.

AMANDA. Oh, fuck. What's happened?

   PHIL *throws himself in a chair.* MARTIN *rips off his coat
   and searches for an address book. He doesn't do either very
   tidily.*

MARTIN. Well, what's happened is, the South African
   ambassador was addressing a meeting of some neo-fascist
   Tory front –

AMANDA. I meant, to Phil –

   She goes to look at PHIL.

MARTIN. Like me, part of a peaceful picket of this noxious
   gathering…

AMANDA. Fuck me.

MARTIN. ...in protest against the upcoming all-white equally neo-fascist Apartheid cricket tour.

AMANDA. Phil, you need to go to hospital.

PHIL. I'm not going to no fucking hospital.

AMANDA *heads to find medication as her daughter,* TANYA, *calls.*

TANYA (*offstage*). Mummy!

AMANDA *is torn, but decides to do* PHIL*'s face first. She takes TCP and cotton wool to him.* MARTIN *has found the address book and is now looking for the phone.*

AMANDA. Well, at least let me try and...

MARTIN. Well, I say 'peaceful', which it was till the stormtroopers of the West Midlands Constabulary decided we were an obstruction to the highway....

MARTIN *has found the phone and is dialling a number.*

AMANDA. Phil, you know, you really should...

MARTIN. And resolved to set Freedom of Assembly back to the eleventh century...

PHIL. Who owns the hospitals?

MARTIN. Hallo?

AMANDA. Well, we do. This may hurt.

MARTIN. Hallo, I need a lawyer.

TANYA (*offstage*). Mummy!

PHIL (*re: the TCP*). Shit.

AMANDA (*re:* PHIL*'s injury*). Christ.

MARTIN (*into phone*). Criminal or civil? Well, that all depends which side...

TANYA (*offstage*). Mummy! Please!

AMANDA. Was anybody busted?

MARTIN. You bet.

(*Into phone*.) Yes I'll hold.

(*To* AMANDA.) With the pigs in hot pursuit.

(*Into phone*.) Yes?

PHIL *is pulling himself away from* AMANDA.

PHIL. I'm going back.

AMANDA. What, you mean they followed you?

TANYA (*offstage*). Mummy!

AMANDA (*to* PHIL). Stay there.

As AMANDA *rushes out:*

MARTIN. Yes, hence my ringing…

PHIL (*stands*). See you.

MARTIN (*into phone*). Hang on.

(*To* PHIL.) Phil, you can't go –

PHIL (*going*). Watch me.

MARTIN (*into phone*). I'll call you back.

He ends the call, dumps the phone on the floor, and chases PHIL.

Look, mate –

He grabs at PHIL, *who turns back*.

PHIL. Four years. Four fucking years. Marching, chanting.
Give peace a fucking chance. Well, a lot of notice taken, eh?
We really had the bastards shaking in their shoes.

MARTIN *tries to take* PHIL *by the arms*.

MARTIN. Okay, mate, but still –

PHIL *pulls away, quite violently*.

PHIL. Hey, you know why there'll never be a revolution in this country? Because the revolutionaries don't think it's going to happen and the only people who do think it's going to happen are the ones who've got the job of fucking stopping it.

Re-enter AMANDA.

AMANDA. Phil –

PHIL. But, oh, we've got The Party. So *that's* all sorted.

MARTIN. Mate, you can't go back –

PHIL. Dead right, mate. I'm never going back. Bombs and bullets, weapons of despair? Tell that to the Panthers and the Vietnamese. 'By any means necessary.' Burn, babies, burn.

PHIL goes quickly out.

AMANDA. Martin.

MARTIN decides. He grabs his coat.

MARTIN. I'm going.

He makes to go. AMANDA *grabs him.*

AMANDA. Martin. No.

MARTIN. You heard him?

AMANDA. Oh, I heard him. 'Bombs and bullets.'

MARTIN (*trying to pull away*). Which actually, on a day like this, is an instinct you can understand –

AMANDA. No, Martin. No.

She faces him.

Today is May Day. We must all remember all the May Days. The days when what we think should happen did. The Paris Commune and the General Strike. The Spanish Republic and Red Barcelona. The Prague Spring and the May events in France.

MARTIN (*turning to go*). Which all flamed out, right?

AMANDA (*pulling him back*). We must remember, we must absolutely not forget, the superhuman things the masses can achieve.

MARTIN pulls away, sits, and lights a cigarette. AMANDA picks up the telephone and dials a number.

MARTIN. Through 'revolutionary discipline'.

AMANDA. And of course the Party isn't always right. But at least we have the tools of understanding *to* be right.

MARTIN. What's this?

AMANDA (*into phone*). Me. Wait.

MARTIN. What's happening?

AMANDA. You're going to be a traitor...

MARTIN. ...to my class.

Pause. MARTIN reaches for the phone. She lifts the receiver and holds it away from him.

AMANDA. And why?

MARTIN. Why?

AMANDA (*still holding it away*). Yes.

Pause.

MARTIN. The West Midlands Constabulary.

AMANDA. And?

MARTIN (*nodding after* PHIL). Not to be like that.

AMANDA. Not now, not ever. And?

MARTIN. Changing human history.

AMANDA (*holding the receiver out to him*). Join, baby, join.

We see JAMES listening on the phone.

Scene Eight

JAMES, MARTIN *and* AMANDA *join the* chorus. *Other members of the* CHORUS *hold up duplicated leaflets.*

CHORUS. Communique Number One. The so-called Marxist parties tell you that the agent of the revolution is the working class. But Marx got it wrong.

MARTIN. June. Tory Edward Heath is elected Prime Minister.

JAMES. Committed to destroying the power of the trade unions.

CHORUS. Communique Number Two. Capitalism has mutated, Now, the theatre of struggle is not the factory but the supermarket. The working class is owned by what it buys.

A BBC outside-broadcast van is bombed, outside the Miss World contest at the Albert Hall.

PHIL *is pulled on to the stage by* POLICEMAN *and manhandled into a chair at a table, as:*

August 1971. Internment without trial is introduced in Northern Ireland.

Opposite PHIL, *a* DETECTIVE *reads from another leaflet:*

DETECTIVE. Communique Number Three. 'The People's Chemistry.' Behind this consumer spectacle there lies an increasingly sophisticated state machine of cooption – co-option – surveillance and repression.

The DETECTIVE *puts a stencil down on* PHIL's *side of the table, so he can read it:*

PHIL (*affecting never to have read this before*). People's Chemistry Communique Number Four. We insist that state actions which perpetuate bad housing, raise rents, and evict the homeless from empty properties, are violent acts. Acts of revolutionary violence against the perpetrators of such actions are thus justified. Not least because they show the people that the state can never be invincible. We are nowhere. We are everywhere.

Pause. PHIL, *with the stencil:*

So I wrote this? You are claiming that I duplicated this? Like, on my duplicator? So what if I did?

DETECTIVE. Well, first, because it locks you into a conspiracy to cause an explosion at the country home of the Minister of State for Housing. And, for two, because it's crazy, Phil.

AMANDA. January 1972. The miners go on strike.

JAMES. And Edward Heath declares a state of emergency.

Blackout.

Scene Nine

JEREMY*'s house in London, February 1972. Darkness – we're in the middle of a power cut.* JEREMY, *now forty-four, appears with a lit candelabra.* MARTIN – *now twenty-six – is there too.*

JEREMY. The university gave it to me. I put it round, I already had a watch.

MARTIN. Yes, I think I get one as an heirloom. So, you're in London now?

JEREMY. Yes. I've a chair at UCL. Would you like a drink?

MARTIN. No thanks. Unless you've got a bitter lemon, or a –

JEREMY. Well, I'm sure I've something on those lines.

JEREMY *goes to the drinks table.*

MARTIN. It's my effort at revolutionary discipline.

JEREMY (*pouring drink*). Oh, yes. I see.

Slight pause.

I don't recall you as a person that amenable to discipline.

MARTIN. Well, people change.

JEREMY. Indeed, they do.

He brings over MARTIN*'s drink.*

So, you're in London too?

MARTIN. That's right. Stoke Newington.

JEREMY. Of course. And did you finish your MA?

MARTIN. Uh – no.

JEREMY. I see. So, what –

MARTIN. Oh, I'm doing it full time.

JEREMY. The revolutionary bit.

MARTIN. That's right. I've got this small trust fund, and it seemed the only thing to do.

JEREMY. Well, it is your money.

MARTIN. Yes, that's what we felt.

JEREMY. Oh, is there a Mrs Glass?

MARTIN. The Party.

The lights come on. JEREMY *lives in a comfortable house, with a studious feel.* MARTIN *takes it in during the following. Now he hands* JEREMY *a copy of* Socialist Vanguard, *the Party paper.*

Please, do have a copy of the paper.

JEREMY. Ah, splendid. Now, you'd be fans of Chairman Mao?

MARTIN. More, Leon Trotsky.

JEREMY (*looking at the paper*). Ah. 'All out for the miners.' That's the coal strike.

MARTIN. Yes?

JEREMY. Oh, and 'Bring the Derry Murderers to justice.' That'll be, the IRA?

MARTIN*'s getting out a cigarette.*

MARTIN. No, that'll be the British paratroops.

JEREMY. And you think that's an argument that cuts the mustard with the British working class?

MARTIN. Why shouldn't it –

JEREMY. I mean, I'd assumed your average flying picket wouldn't give the time of day to an Irish psychopath, or would he? I merely ask for information.

Pause.

Your cigarette's the wrong way round.

Which it is. MARTIN *reverses it.*

MARTIN. Yes, I think you're right. But, it's remarkable how fast things move. I mean, who'd have thought a year ago, eleven thousand engineers, all over Birmingham, would down tools, march across the city, close down a coke depot, and maybe win a miners' strike? Who would have believed the poor old working class, written off by everybody, with their Hoovers and their tellies, passive and inert, would actually, suddenly, behave like heroes?

JEREMY. Ah, yes, is it not Lennon who reminds us –

MARTIN. And who's to say, in twelve months' time, they wouldn't do the same to get British imperialism out of Ireland. I'm sorry. You were saying. Lenin.

JEREMY. Lenn*on*, actually.

He notes that MARTIN*'s glass is still full. He goes to help himself.*

Forgive me. Whenever I hear the word 'imperialism', I reach straight for the bottle. John Lennon, isn't it?

MARTIN. What is?

JEREMY. 'A working-class hero's something to be'?

He stands, sipping his drink.

Why did you come and see me?

MARTIN. I'm sorry, I don't know what's happened.

JEREMY. Well, you rang up, and you asked me if I'd mind –

MARTIN. I meant, to you.

Pause.

JEREMY. You could say, I was brutally assaulted by the real world.

MARTIN. I have a friend who was brutally assaulted by the real police.

JEREMY. I'm sorry.

MARTIN. And has just been jailed for ten years.

JEREMY. Good God. Whatever for?

MARTIN. For running off a stencil on his duplicator.

JEREMY. Oh, yes. The bombings trial. The – 'People's Chemistry'? They tried to blow up, what was it? A cottage in the Cotswolds? Belonging to some ludicrously junior Minister of State?

MARTIN. Yes, Hugh Trelawney. Man who wrote the Housing Bill.

Slight pause.

There's an appeal. And a campaign. And that's actually why I came to see you.

Pause.

JEREMY. Oh. Oh, dear.

MARTIN. It being thought, in fact by me, distinguished man of letters, record of support for various progressive causes... silly of me.

JEREMY. Well, you really should read other newspapers.

Slight pause.

I'm sorry. How embarrassing for you. D'you think he's innocent, your friend?

MARTIN. I've really no idea.

JEREMY. I've just stopped being sorry.

MARTIN. Was there a moment? Road to Damascus, sudden burst of light?

JEREMY. No, I don't think so...

MARTIN. No waking one morning and, guess what, why don't we sell off all the council houses? Send the blacks home? Bomb Russia?

JEREMY. Well, I did decide to drop all that tramping through the rain.

MARTIN. D'you miss it?

JEREMY. Not a jot.

MARTIN. And then?

JEREMY. Well, if you insist, I think there was a Kronstadt moment. Kronstadt?

MARTIN. Sailors' uprising against the Bolsheviks. Petrograd. 1921.

JEREMY. Put down by your hero Trotsky, as it happens.

MARTIN. And the 'moment'?

JEREMY. Oh, I assumed you knew. It's the moment when you realise the revolution has eaten its own children. Whether Kronstadt, or the purges and the show trials in the thirties. Or Hungary.

MARTIN. Yes, well, we've no / truck with –

JEREMY. While for me it was an incident in October 1969. At Leeds University. And the issue was – I think a visitor whose views weren't to the student taste... And I thought, oh, here we go again. Banning, purging, Party lines. The same philistine distrust of anything that challenged, anything that didn't fit. And I thought, oh, come on, Jeremy: this isn't what you meant at all.

MARTIN. Well, it may not have been what *you* / meant –

JEREMY. And then I learned about a Russian dissident called
Lermontov – ordinary chap, in what you'd doubtless call a
bourgeois occupation – who'd been arrested for the crime of
circulating a petition. A petition, I may say, not concerned
with the right of people to throw bombs at members of the
government, or even dump their garbage in my office, but
about the right to public demonstration, a privilege which in
this country is as you know quite reverently protected.

MARTIN. Not in my experience.

JEREMY. The man was sentenced to five years, in a labour
camp, For 'discrediting the system'. And then he smuggled
out a statement from the camps, about the camps. And was
sentenced to another ten. For 'agitation to subvert the state'.
And I thought, now, that's the type of man that I admire. I'm
with the malcontents and the subversives. I don't think I've
changed.

Pause.

MARTIN. Well, I'm naturally very sorry.

JEREMY. Naturally.

MARTIN. But one thing's clear, at least.

JEREMY. What's that?

MARTIN. 'A middle-class hero is something to be.'

Pause.

JEREMY. Yes, you know the only thing you've said that gives
me any hope at all?

MARTIN. What's that?

JEREMY. That this bomber is your friend. Because that means
that your love for the whole of humankind has not yet
strangled, quite, your capacity to love the people whom you
actually know.

MARTIN. That's hope for what?

JEREMY. That you'll get out, before it does.

MARTIN. I ought to get out now.

JEREMY. But, still, you're very welcome –

MARTIN. You know, Jeremy, I think the real problem is, you feel the working class has let you down.

JEREMY. What, by not all turning into Michelangelos?

MARTIN. No, the reverse. For not being proper victims. Being uppity. Fighting for their rights. Not tugging forelocks. Like your students. I do think that's the problem, really.

JEREMY. While for you, of course, the problem comes – will come – when the oppressed stop being heroes.

MARTIN. Who?

JEREMY. Well, I don't know, the Viet Cong, the miners, your bomb-throwing friend – who else are you hero-worshipping today?

MARTIN stands, puts on his coat.

Apparently, they say that in the labour camps… somewhere in that wilderness… there's still a prisoner who fought at Kronstadt. Fifty years.

Slight pause.

MARTIN. Yes. You know what strikes me, Jeremy?

JEREMY. What's that?

MARTIN. That I was wrong.

JEREMY. Well, mercy.

MARTIN. That the thing that really fucks you off is that you weren't a Red *at Trinity*. To be quite frank, sir. Bye.

He goes out. JEREMY *raises his glass. We see* LERMONTOV, *in prison uniform. Then we hear Prime Minister Edward Heath, announcing a general election:*

EDWARD HEATH. As many of you will have heard, Her
Majesty agreed today to my request that Parliament should
be dissolved. The issue before you is a simple one… Do you
want a government that will abandon the struggle against
rising prices under pressure from one particular powerful
group of workers?

Scene Ten

Outside a meeting hall in London, early February 1974. The
CHORUS *has become six* PAPERSELLERS, *forming a line-up*
to the door of the meeting hall. PEOPLE *attending the meeting*
thus have to run a kind of gauntlet. MARTIN *walks towards the*
door. Everyone is muffled up against the cold.

1ST PAPERSELLER. *The Workers' Week*! Kick out the Tories!

2ND PAPERSELLER. *The Revolutionary Worker*! Vote Labour
on Feb 28th!

3RD PAPERSELLER. *The Revolutionary Marxist Worker*!
Back the Miners' Strike!

4TH PAPERSELLER. *Socialist Vanguard*! Build the
Revolutionary Moment!

5TH PAPERSELLER. *Morning Star*?

MARTIN *turns to the* 5TH PAPERSELLER, *giving the* 6TH
PAPERSELLER *no chance to promote his/her wares.*

MARTIN. No thanks. If I want to do a crossword, then I'll buy
The Times. Hey, James!

6TH PAPERSELLER. Um –

MARTIN *has seen* JAMES *enter. He hurries over.*

JAMES. Ah, Martin, how –

MARTIN. James, I need to talk to you.

1ST PAPERSELLER. *The Workers' Week*. Kick out the Tories.

JAMES. *The Worker's Fortnight*, soon, I hear.

MARTIN. My paper, for the internal bulletin. On the current party-building strategy.

JAMES. Yes, what about it?

2ND PAPERSELLER. *The Revolutionary Worker*. For socialism and a Labour Victory.

JAMES. Make up your mind, I'll buy the paper.

MARTIN. You rejected it.

JAMES. The political committee rejected it.

MARTIN. And why?

3RD PAPERSELLER. *The Revolutionary Marxist Worker*. The paper that supports the miners.

JAMES. Well, you shatter me.

4TH PAPERSELLER. *Socialist Vanguard*?

MARTIN. Thank you, we subscribe.

JAMES. Well, there was the matter of the paper.

MARTIN. And the Party's policy to turn it into *The Beano*.

JAMES. Or put another way, the editorial committee's quite correct decision not to publish long and tortuous articles by you about friends of yours in jail for acts of individual terrorism.

5TH PAPERSELLER. *The Morning Star*?

JAMES. No, thank you. When I want a recipe, I buy the *Guardian*.

MARTIN. He was – he is a revolutionary.

JAMES. He may think he is a revolutionary. Objectively, he is nothing of the kind.

MARTIN. 'Objectively.'

6TH PAPERSELLER. Um –

MARTIN *grabs* JAMES*'s arm and pulls him back:*

MARTIN. Look. I won't resign.

JAMES. I rather doubt that there'll be any need.

MARTIN. I beg your pardon?

JAMES. The political committee is considering its position on the rightward-leaning elements within the Party. Elements like you.

MARTIN. You can't be serious.

JAMES (*suddenly angry*). Martin, it's very simple. There are things you're not prepared to sacrifice. There is something in you that fundamentally distrusts the concept of a leadership, particularly if it's on the surface less articulate than you.

MARTIN. You mean, you're purging me?

JAMES *shrugs and turns.*

Look. Look. I stopped. I pulled out of the Phil Mandrell Support Group. I did what I was told.

JAMES. Reluctantly.

MARTIN. It was a very bad time. The appeal was just beginning.

JAMES. As was the second national miners' strike in two years.

MARTIN. And actually, we were right. He got off.

JAMES. On a technicality.

MARTIN. And, yes, he is my friend.

JAMES. Well, as I said, / that's –

MARTIN. And don't you feel that matters?

JAMES. What, that he's your / friend?

MARTIN. Comradeship? Solidarity? Behaving like the change
we want to bring about? I mean, just a little? And act the way
we feel?

JAMES. As I've said before, I couldn't care less what you feel.
It's what you think and do. And what your present thoughts
are doing is to undermine the seizing of the time through
which we are passing at the moment, which is principally
defined by the fact that the working class appears to be
bringing down the Government.

I'm sorry, Martin, but that's all.

JAMES *goes quickly through the door into the meeting.*

6TH PAPERSELLER. Um –

MARTIN *following as the lights dim and the setting begins
to change.*

Stick-Up? For Brighter Revolutions?

MARTIN *stops.*

MARTIN. Christ. Are you still going?

6TH PAPERSELLER. Strong.

MARTIN. Then, yes.

(*Fumbling for change.*) Yes, please...

AMANDA *enters, as the scene continues to transform into...*

Scene Eleven

A communal house in Notting Hill, February 1974. AMANDA *has admitted* MARTIN.

AMANDA. So what did you expect?

MARTIN. Well, not a gold watch, I suppose.

AMANDA. I'm sorry?

MARTIN. Look, I don't suppose you've got a / drink –

AMANDA (*nodding*). Take your coat off and sit down.

> AMANDA *finds a half-bottle of Scotch and pours drinks for both of them.* MARTIN *takes off his coat and sits on the arm of a chair.* AMANDA *taps her shoulder.*

Well, here it is.

> MARTIN *looks at her and smiles.*

MARTIN. Do you know what struck me? Very forcibly? I've spent four years of patient toil, trying to make Socialist Vanguard the government. And I looked at him, as he put the knife in me, with all the tact and understated charm of Vlad the Impaler, and thought: come on, do you really want this man to run the country?

> *Slight pause.*

AMANDA. And now he's dumped us both.

MARTIN (*clicking*). Oh, yeah.

AMANDA. Well, hon, I'm full of sympathy, but if you ask me, you're well out of it. When I left my feelings were of pure relief. No more, the desperate scramble through the paper, trying to suss out this month's line. In my time, I took up more positions than the Kama Sutra.

MARTIN. You jumped. I was pushed.

> *Slight pause.*

And then, today of all days… when the working class is actually behaving in a way that Marx and Lenin said it would, seizing history by the throat, when our fucking rhetoric comes real…

Pause.

AMANDA. It's not the end.

Slight pause.

Why should it be the end? Why should 'The Party' be the only place to be?

MARTIN. You've changed your tune. What about the 'tools of understanding'?

AMANDA. Pretty limited, I realised. What about the planet? What about the person?

MARTIN. It was Phil. It was me supporting Phil.

AMANDA. Well, intermittently.

Pause.

In fact, hon, he's involved / with –

Suddenly, MARTIN *jumps up.*

MARTIN. Well, here you are. In your collective living situation. Building little islands of pure socialism, within the capitalist sea.

AMANDA. Well, trying to live the revolution. Trying to be the change we want bring about.

MARTIN. No purges. No 'objectively'.

AMANDA. No chance.

MARTIN. So where's the gang?

AMANDA. There's a squat in Lissom Grove. The pigs gave notice of a bust, and everybody's round there, manning barricades.

MARTIN. And you?

AMANDA. I'm kind of, base camp?

MARTIN. Ah. I see.

Slight pause.

AMANDA. Have you no other shoulder?

MARTIN. Why, do you want me to...

AMANDA. No, no. Just wondered.

MARTIN (*slightly blurted*). Look, look, Mand – would you like to go out? For a meal, or something? Talk of old times, weep into our rogan josh?

AMANDA. Martin, I am in charge of three small / children –

MARTIN. Then tomorrow, when the gang's all back?

Pause.

AMANDA. No, tomorrow there's a tenants' meeting.

MARTIN. Friday?

AMANDA. Women's group.

MARTIN. The weekend?

AMANDA. I would have to check, but I think we're blocking Westway.

MARTIN. Mand. How can I put this?

Slight pause.

Rearrange the following into a well-known phrase or saying... Something I've You Always Rotten Fancied.

Pause.

AMANDA. Beg pardon?

MARTIN (*going to* AMANDA). You know, the game like, um, 'Glass Shouldn't People Stones In Houses Throw'.

AMANDA. Yes, I got that.

MARTIN. Well?

AMANDA. Glass Shouldn't. I should not with Glass.

Pause.

MARTIN. Why not?

AMANDA. All sorts of reasons. Theoretical and practical.

MARTIN. Let's start with practice.

AMANDA. Never on a rebound.

MARTIN. I'm not on a rebound.

AMANDA. No?

Long pause

MARTIN. The best years of my life.

AMANDA says nothing. MARTIN finds the bottle, and pours himself another Scotch. His hands are shaking.

And now – I'm nothing.

AMANDA. You're not nothing.

MARTIN. But –

AMANDA. As long as you don't kill off the bit of you you value most.

MARTIN. What's that?

AMANDA. Martin, I used to cry –

Suddenly, a group of LIBERTARIANS – people living in or connected with the house – burst in. Some wear scarves or other things masking their faces. One carries a crying baby.

1ST LIBERTARIAN. Well, good evening, merry campers. And welcome to the non-stop Revolutionary Cock-Up Show.

AMANDA. What happened?

People rushing around, looking for things, tending wounds.

2ND LIBERTARIAN. They got the fucking time wrong, didn't they? When we arrived the pigs were already there.

(*To the crying baby*.) Choo choo. Be quiet, baby.

AMANDA. What, in the house?

1ST LIBERTARIAN. All over it. The silly fuckers didn't change the locks.

2ND LIBERTARIAN. Rule One. Change all the locks.

AMANDA. Um, Mart...

2ND LIBERTARIAN. Choo choo.

MARTIN (*to* AMANDA). Was this – a real family?

AMANDA. Yes. It was a real, kosher, working-class and homeless, family. Where's Mother?

2ND LIBERTARIAN. In the pig-pen. She went all hysterical.

Enter PHIL, *with a scarf across his face*.

1ST LIBERTARIAN. Rule Two.

PHIL. Do Not Go All Hysterical.

MARTIN *recognises* PHIL.

MARTIN. Phil?

PHIL *takes off his face-scarf*.

AMANDA. I tried to tell you.

MARTIN. Um – how are you?

PHIL. Well, I'm out of jail.

MARTIN. Yes, I'm very pleased.

PHIL. No thanks to you.

1ST LIBERTARIAN. Who's that?

MARTIN. That isn't really fair.

PHIL. It's Martin Glass.

The 1ST LIBERTARIAN *knows the significance of the name, but not the* 2ND LIBERTARIAN, *so the* 1ST LIBERTARIAN *whispers:*

1ST LIBERTARIAN. SV.

PHIL. Who offered us his help. To promote my case.

AMANDA. Who gave his help.

During this, the baby starts crying again and the 2ND
LIBERTARIAN *takes her out.*

PHIL. Until The Party tells him I'm 'objectively' a petit-
bourgeois adventurist. And suddenly, in the middle of a
criminal appeal, when he might have been some use,
Comrade Glass goes all transparent, and you cannot see him
any more.

MARTIN. Well, as I say, I don't / think that's –

PHIL. I mean, we've had time together, Comrade Glass and me.
You'd think that that would count for something.

AMANDA. Phil –

PHIL. But, then there are things the comrade can't give up. Like
he has this real problem working in a group that isn't *led*. Or,
if it is, is led by everyone.

MARTIN. Please. Please, don't tell me what I think.

PHIL. Oh, there's nothing wrong with what you think, mate. It's
what you don't appear to feel.

AMANDA. Phil. He left the Party, over his support for you.

PHIL. Oh, did he? When?

MARTIN. Too late.

PHIL. Now, we need to get Mum out of the pig-pen.

MARTIN. Can I help?

PHIL looks witheringly at MARTIN, *and goes.*

The 1ST LIBERTARIAN *follows* PHIL *out.*

Thank you.

AMANDA. You know, I could – it might be possible to skip the
tenants' group.

The 2ND LIBERTARIAN *appears with the crying baby.*

2ND LIBERTARIAN. Could someone. There's no milk. Could someone go...

AMANDA (*moving*). Yuh. Sure.

AMANDA *goes out. As the scene splits and changes,* MARTIN *stays holding his glass of whisky. We hear a grossly inadequate rendition of 'Good King Wenceslas'.*

Scene Twelve

A country vicarage, Christmas Eve, 1974. A comfortable but rather empty room. A little Christmas tree. MARTIN *stands with his glass of Scotch. The carol stops. Pause. Enter* MRS GLASS, MARTIN's *mother.* MARTIN *looks at her.*

MRS GLASS. It wasn't carol singers. just three grubby boys.

MARTIN. Oh? It sounded like –

MRS GLASS. Not proper carol singers.

MARTIN. Did you give them anything?

MRS GLASS. Oh, no. I ask them if they're collecting, for some charity, and if they say 'no', I don't give a thing. I mean, it's actually begging, isn't it?

Pause.

It starts in mid-November. Actually, I blame the parents.

She goes and pours herself a glass of Madeira.

Do you want another Madeira?

MARTIN. No. I'm drinking Scotch.

MRS GLASS. Well, you can help yourself then.

MARTIN *does so.*

There used to be the proper carol singers. From the church. With horns and bells. And not just carols either. Real wassailing songs. They'd carry lanterns and we'd have them in. It was bliss.

MARTIN (*under his breath*). Oh, Jesus.

Pause.

MRS GLASS. So you've got a proper job now?

MARTIN. Yes, if you can call the *Islington and Hackney Messenger* a proper job.

MRS GLASS. And you've moved.

MARTIN. Into a state of unwed bliss with a single mother. Yes.

MRS GLASS *does not look at him.*

How long do you keep the vicarage?

MRS GLASS. Oh, just till the New Year, actually. It's kind of them, to let me stay for Christmas. It's been ten months, after all.

MARTIN. New vicar moving in?

MRS GLASS. Oh, no. Nice couple. He's a – captain? Or a 'lieutenant', anyway. But she's British. No, the parish shares a vicar now.

Pause.

I suppose it doesn't really matter. Last real Christmas that we'll have. I think, don't you? Before the whole thing falls about our ears.

MARTIN. The whole thing whats?

MRS GLASS. Now Labour's back in. And your unions straining at the leash to bring the whole thing crashing down.

MARTIN. Now, Mother, you must stop all that. You know it's only wishful thinking. Wanting it so badly won't bring it any closer.

MRS GLASS *looks at* MARTIN. *Pause.*

MRS GLASS. Do you want to come to Midnight Mass?

MARTIN. I thought you said –

MRS GLASS. Oh, it's here this year. It's on a kind of rota, actually.

MARTIN. Yes, if you like.

MRS GLASS. I do.

Pause.

I was clearing out some rubbish in the attic, actually. I was thinking about other Christmas Eves. You and your father sledging in the afternoon. In with a shiver, to the smell of woodsmoke. Mince pies and mulled claret. And at nearly midnight, crunch across the snow.

I found the crib you and your father made. We've lost a wise man and the ox. And Joseph, actually.

MARTIN. Oh, Mother, please, do stop.

MRS GLASS. Stop what?

MARTIN. Saying 'actually' in every sentence.

Slight pause.

Sorry.

MRS GLASS. I didn't know I was.

MARTIN. It never was like that.

MRS GLASS. You won't remember.

MARTIN. Yes I do.

Slight pause.

I remember, every year, three gruesome days of attempting to pretend we were a Christmas card. A kind of séance, trying to raise the nineteenth century. Oh, are you out there, jolly red-faced coachman? Oh, can you hear us, Tiny Tim?

But then it was Mother's little yearly treat. Playing at mistress of the manor. With her scarves and wellingtons and fucking mulled red wine.

MRS GLASS *looks away.*

What I do remember, coming back from school, on that grimy, drafty train, was fantasising how I'd shock the pants off you this year. What I would do or say. To really sear your mind.

MRS GLASS. I know. 'Up the workers, down the bourgeoisie.' He did that too.

Pause. MARTIN *goes and fills up his drink.*

MARTIN. Who did it too?

MRS GLASS. Your father. And I sometimes thought, if you had to use the Kenwood or the tumble dryer, you might be a bit less snooty about those of us who do.

Slight pause.

MARTIN. What do you mean?

MRS GLASS. Oh, Martin. He'd remark, when I'd worked at something, obviously, all day, at baking, sewing something for the parish: 'Of course, the whole thing's nonsense, isn't it? It's all the silliest pretence, to stop the silliest of people facing up to what's real in their lives.'

While in fact of course it's actually a way of facing up to things. And it always struck me that you had to be quite silly not to spot that, really. People wanting to belong to something. To be loyal to it. Even die for it.

MRS GLASS *goes and puts the top back on the whisky.*

And your father, of all people. Going on about pretence. You know, he used to cross his fingers when he sang 'I Vow to Thee, My Country'?

But there was always the promise of 'the New Jerusalem'. Somewhere. Nowhere.

While the ordinary people –

MARTIN. Dust.

MRS GLASS. I beg your pardon?

MARTIN. It's a phrase of Trotsky's.

MRS GLASS. Trotsky.

MARTIN. Human dust.

A long pause. Then MARTIN *moves downstage. It's as if he's looking into a mirror.*

You see, I just...

Pause.

I just no longer can believe...

Pause.

That a third of humankind...

AMANDA *appears behind him. She's dressed for a party. She carries a bottle.*

AMANDA. Is what?

MARTIN. I'm sorry?

AMANDA. 'A third of humankind' is what?

MARTIN. Uh – nothing.

AMANDA. Lovey, are you okay?

MARTIN. I'm cool.

AMANDA. 'It's nothing.' 'Cool.' We ought to go.

She goes out.

MARTIN. That a third of humankind is living in an aberration. Or to be required by anybody to believe... that *anyone*...

Scene Thirteen

A private house in North London. A party, at which MARTIN *and* AMANDA *have just arrived.*

CHORUS. May Day, 1975.

NBC NEWS. The Communist forces, some of them riding in Russian-made tanks, some in captured American jeeps, rolled into Saigon about three and a half hours after the dramatic evacuation of the US nationals and many south Vietnamese.

AMANDA. D'you want to get some food?

MARTIN. No, first things first. I never eat on an empty liver.

AMANDA. Fine.

   MARTIN *goes off in search of glasses, as* AMANDA *spots* JUDY, *now in her early thirties, and crosses to her. On his way out,* MARTIN *passes a conversation between a male* SMOKER *and a female non-smoking partygoer, called* MOLLY.

SMOKER. Well, I can't see how it's a class question.

MOLLY. Well, what about what the tobacco companies are up to in the third world.

SMOKER. I'm not in the third world. I'm in Muswell Hill.

   MARTIN *returns with two beakers of wine. He stops to overhear.*

MOLLY. But the thing I found most telling was your remark that you smoke at meetings because you're nervous and you're bored.

SMOKER. Well, I didn't quite / put it that –

MOLLY. And it seems to me you're nervous because you're working out some devastating speech, to impress your friends, and you're bored because you never listen to what anybody else has got to say. So if it isn't about class, then it's absolutely about gender. No?

She turns and goes. The SMOKER *is left there. He has half an inch of ash, can't see an ashtray. He flicks the ash into his jacket pocket.*

MARTIN (*to* JUDY *and* AMANDA). My God, it's like St Crispin's Day back there.

AMANDA. What do you mean?

MARTIN. Revolutionary nostalgia, rampant in the kitchen. With reference the victory of the triumphant Vietnamese. And everybody's part in bringing it about.

AMANDA. Now, Martin, you remember Judy?

MARTIN. Yes, of course. Are you still in the / RMF –

JUDY. No. I'm in the Labour Party.

MARTIN. Heavens. Jude, sustaining the illusions of the working class in the parliamentary road?

JUDY. Well, that's not how I'd put it.

MARTIN. No?

JUDY. I'd put it as recapturing the party of the working class for the principles of socialism.

MARTIN. But you don't think that, in fact the fundamental role of parties like the Labour Party has been precisely to prevent the working class from the achievement of its socialist aspirations, by deviating their mass action down the channels of…

Pause.

The channels of –

JUDY (*to* AMANDA). Um?

MARTIN. Sorry, it's completely gone.

JUDY. What's gone?

MARTIN. I can't remember what comes next. No matter.
Bound to come back to me.

He smiles. His glass is empty.

I think I'm going to try and liberate our bottle.

He goes. Pause.

JUDY. So… how do you feel about the referendum?

AMANDA. Sorry?

JUDY. The Common Market referendum?

AMANDA. I'm sorry, Jude. Excuse me.

She catches MARTIN up.

Martin, what's wrong?

MARTIN. There's nothing wrong.

AMANDA. That is palpably not true.

MARTIN looks at her and goes out. She returns to JUDY.

JUDY. Is he all right?

AMANDA. I'm sorry. He's thirty tomorrow, and taking the
whole thing very badly.

JUDY. Are you two – I didn't think, in Birmingham…

AMANDA. No, a recent development. Oh, hell the what, say I.

JUDY. Sorry?

JAMES comes to AMANDA.

JAMES. Amanda.

AMANDA. James.

*MARTIN has re-entered with a bottle of wine. He is
smoking. He stumbles slightly, nearly into MOLLY, who's in
conversation.*

MARTIN. Excuse me. Sorry.

MOLLY. Please, don't smoke that thing at me.

JAMES. A great day.

AMANDA. Yes.

> MARTIN *turns back*.

MARTIN. Uh – are you talking to me?

MOLLY. Fuck off.

MARTIN. You what?

MOLLY (*turning back to her conversation*). You heard.

> MARTIN *to* JAMES, AMANDA *and* BRYONY, *as:*

JAMES (*raising his glass*). So, May Day. To the defeat of US imperialism. To the victory of the heroic Vietnamese.

> AMANDA *and* BRYONY *raise their glasses as* MARTIN *arrives. He pulls* AMANDA *a little away from the rest of the group*.

MARTIN (*pointing to* MOLLY). Who is that woman?

AMANDA. Molly Something. Wages for Housework, I believe.

MARTIN. Really? In fact, I think my mother feels –

AMANDA. Martin, right now, I'm not that interested in what you think.

MARTIN. No, it's what my mother / feels –

AMANDA. Or what you feel.

MARTIN. I'm sorry?

AMANDA. Or even, at this moment, though I think it might be crucial, actually, to what you are.

MARTIN. To what I am?

> JAMES *approaches*.

JAMES. Ah, Martin.

MARTIN. James. So, let me guess the Party Line. The Vietnamese are selling out already?

JAMES. No, we unconditionally welcome the heroic victory /
of the –

MARTIN. Of course. The routing of US imperialism. 'By any
means necessary.'

AMANDA. Martin –

MARTIN. This despite all those renegades and Trotskyites
liquidated by Ho Chi Minh.

JAMES. Well, we obviously acknowledge there are
contradictions.

MARTIN. So your actual prediction, for revolutionary
Vietnam? Another Stalinist degeneration? Yet another
population frogmarched into labour camps? Another
revolution eating its own children?

JAMES. Well, I wouldn't be surprised if there were /
similarities –

MARTIN. I think in five years' time we will all cringe at the
memory of tonight.

*Pause. A few people have heard this. The buzz of
conversation dying, as:*

At least, I hope so. Cringe and blush and fidget. Try to
change the subject. Hope we will.

AMANDA. Martin.

*Almost everyone now listening. The odd laugh, as if it's a
joke.*

MARTIN. When this great socialist experiment goes all wrong
too. And the walls are built and the barbed wire is in place
and the secret police are busy secret policing, and anyone
who can is trying to escape… I hope we'll cringe. Don't
you?

Silence.

JAMES. Oh, dear.

MARTIN. But I doubt it. What I imagine will occur is another alibi, like the last time, and the time before, you've got to factor in the ravages of war, you can't build socialism in one country...

MOLLY. Who is this prick?

MOLLY leaves.

MARTIN. And as once again the proofs pile up that we are catastrophically wrong, we change the question. Or indeed, having predicted that the world will definitely end on Tuesday, we spend Wednesday morning arguing that all this proves is that the apocalypse is bound to roll along by the weekend. That all these 'actually existing' workers' states, all these Democratic Republics of Misnomer, that *they're* the deviation, and that therefore somewhere in the future there must be a norm.

SMOKER. Bullshit.

He goes out.

MARTIN. So I'm sorry, but I just no longer can believe, that a third of humankind is living in an aberration.

AMANDA. Ah.

MARTIN. Any more than I believe the workers of the West are straining at the leash to bite their way to Communism, if only we could crack the chains that bind them to their Kenwoods and their Hoover Automatics.

You see, I don't think it's just Stalin, or even Lenin. I think it is the whole idea.

(*To* AMANDA.) That there's no morality except the interests of the revolution, that to be a revolutionary you must purge yourself of the bits of you you value most.

And what's it all for, in the end? What is this 'true socialism' that's lurking in our heads, because it's surely nowhere else, what's it actually like? I mean, really?

AMANDA puts her hand on MARTIN's arm.

AMANDA. Mart. Please.

MARTIN (*pulling his arm away*). It's a Golden Age. Utopia.
   It's nowhere. And, for the sake of that, I don't believe, I can't
   believe, I actually refuse to be required by anybody to
   believe, that anyone is human dust.

   Pause.

   So does anyone agree with anything of this? No? Nothing?
   Well, it's what I think and feel.

   They say that every generation has its Kronstadt moment.
   Well, today is mine. No more pretence.

   I feel a great deal better.

   MARTIN *goes quickly out.*

AMANDA. Well, I suppose. It's only rock'n'roll.

   Enter LERMONTOV, *in an ill-fitting overcoat and a hat. He
   is forty-nine.*

Scene Fourteen

*Late 1978. The snow-covered Glienicke Bridge across the
Havel river, linking the German Democratic Republic with the
westernmost point of West Berlin. There is a white line painted
across the bridge at its mid-point. Searchlights and* SNIPERS
above.

At the GDR end, a female KGB OFFICER *brings* LERMONTOV
forward towards the white line. The British AMBASSADOR *to
the GDR brings a female spy,* SVETLANA DANILOVA, *to the
same point on the other side of the line. With him is a forty-three-
year-old Hungarian called* MIKLOS PALOCZI.

AMBASSADOR (*identifying the spy*). Svetlana Danilova.

KGB OFFICER (*Russian*). *Snimitye shlyapu.* [Take off your hat.]

DANILOVA does so. The KGB OFFICER *checks a photograph, then nods 'Okay'.* DANILOVA *makes to move, but the* AMBASSADOR *interrupts.*

AMBASSADOR. Wait.

He turns and gestures PALOCZI *forward.*

(*To* LERMONTOV.) Please, would you remove your hat?

LERMONTOV *does that, revealing his prison haircut. The* AMBASSADOR *turns to* PALOCZI.

Well?

PALOCZI (*English*). Yes. This is Pavel Lermontov.

The AMBASSADOR *turns to the* KGB OFFICER *and nods.*

KGB OFFICER (*Russian*). *Idyom.* [Let's go.]

LERMONTOV *and* DANILOVA *walk slowly towards each other. Suddenly,* LERMONTOV *panics and stops. The* SNIPERS *take aim.*

LERMONTOV (*in accented English*). And who is this man?

PALOCZI. Miklos Paloczi. Hungary, 1956.

Slight pause.

'The revolution is a festival.' Don't you remember?

He opens his arms.

Pavel.

DANILOVA *hurries to the* KGB OFFICER. LERMONTOV *goes to* PALOCZI.

LERMONTOV. Paloczi. Oh, yes.

They embrace.

(*Overwelmed.*) Oh yes. Oh yes.

PALOZCI. Welcome.

End of Part One.

Part Two

A number of Western commentators have stressed the role of the 'generation gap' in the rise of Soviet dissent. According to this theory, dissent is largely the work of the post-war generation. This younger generation was shocked and repelled by the revelations of its parents' complicity, whether active or passive, in Stalin's repressions... From this perspective, Soviet dissent may appear to be a local branch of the world-wide youth rebellion of the late sixties.

Marshall S. Shatz, *Soviet Dissent: Historical Perspectives*

From Lenin I went back to the Russian thinkers of the nineteenth century, and stumbled across an amusing characteristic of theirs: all of them, sitting on their estates or in their city flats, loved to hold forth about the people, about the latent unplumbed forces of the people and about how the people would one day awaken from their slumbers and resolve everything, pronounce the ultimate truth, and create a genuine culture... To us who had grown up in the communal backyards of this selfsame proletariat, living among them as equals, not masters, the term 'proletarian culture' sounded grotesque.

Vladimir Bukovsky (Soviet dissident),
To Build a Castle, 1978

The defence of individual rights has reached such an extreme that society itself is becoming defenceless against certain individuals. And in the West it is high time to defend, not so much the rights of the individuals, as their duties.

Alexander Solzhenitsyn (Soviet dissident),
Harvard speech, 1978

Scene One

*A military barracks in Budapest, 5 November 1956. In an outer
area, with one* SOVIET SOLDIER *by the exit, and a*
SERGEANT *by a bench.*

*A little office area, with a table and three chairs, on one of
which a Soviet Army stenographer,* CLARA IVANOVNA, *sits
typing. On her table are a pile of files, a cardboard box, and a
radio, from which an operetta tune is emanating. There is a side
exit to the street.*

*As the scene gathers, we hear a mosaic of broadcasts from the
day of the Soviet invasion of Hungary, 4 November 1956:*

BBC BROADCAST. It's Sunday, the 4th of November 1956.
The Soviet air force has bombed part of the Hungarian
capital, Budapest, and Russian troops have poured into the
city in a massive dawn offensive. At least one thousand
Soviet tanks are reported to have entered Budapest and
troops deployed throughout the country are battling with
Hungarian forces for strategic positions.

The words of IMRE NAGY, *Hungarian prime minister:*

IMRE NAGY. Today at daybreak, Soviet troops attacked our
capital with the obvious intent of overthrowing the legal
democratic Hungarian government. I notify the people of our
country and the entire world of this fact.

Hungarian broadcast:

HUNGARIAN. Civilised people of the world. On the watch
tower of one-thousand-year-old Hungary the last flames
begin to go out. Soviet tanks and guns are roaring over
Hungarian soil. Our women – mothers and daughters – are
sitting in dread. They still have terrible memories of the
army's entry in 1945. Save our souls.

A proclamation in the streets of Budapest:

SOVIET UNION. At the request of the Hungarian revolutionary government of workers and peasants, the Soviet army has temporarily moved into Budapest in order to extend fraternal help in defending the socialist achievements of the Hungarian people, overcoming the counter-revolution, and in warding off the danger of fascism.

Another Hungarian broadcast:

2ND HUNGARIAN. This word may be the last from the last Hungarian freedom station. Listen to our call. Help us – not with advice, not with words, but with action, with soldiers and arms.

A broadcast recorded by the head of the Hungarian Writers' Union 'in all the languages he knows':

WRITERS' UNION. This is the Hungarian Writers' Union. We are appealing for help to writers, scholars, writers' organisations, academies, scientific organisations, the leaders of intellectual life all over the world. Our time is limited! You all know the facts, there is no need to explain them. Help Hungary! Help the Hungarian people! Help the Hungarian writers, scholars, workers, peasants and intellectuals! Help! Help! Help!

The voice of the young PALOCZI, *broadcasting over shortwave radio:*

PALOCZI. Comrades, take care! Counter-revolutionaries are everywhere. No less than ten million landowners and capitalists and bishops roam the country, laying waste to all that they survey. Even the strongholds of the proletariat have not escaped infection. Forty thousand aristocrats and fascists are on strike in Csepel, aided and abetted by the forces of imperialism. Comrades, vigilance! Socialism is in danger!

A prisoner (PALOCZI, *now twenty-one*) *is marched in by another* SOLDIER.

1ST SOLDIER. At the double, move move move.

SERGEANT. Name.

PALOCZI *doesn't reply.*

Name!

PALOCZI. Paloczi, Miklos.

SERGEANT. Sit. Hands on head.

He does so, as LERMONTOV *comes into the office, from a side entrance. He is now twenty-seven.* CLARA *stands quickly; after a moment, she switches off the radio.*

LERMONTOV. You like operetta, comrade?

CLARA (*after a second*). Oh yes, comrade lieutenant, very much. Do you?

LERMONTOV. Well, yes, yes.

He looks in the cardboard box. It is full of the paraphernalia of urban guerrilla war: broken milk bottles, oily rags, a piece of chain, a flick-knife, a hammer, a couple of hand grenades. As he does so, a 2ND SOLDIER *marches another prisoner* (ERICA MOLNAR), *into the outer area, as the* 1ST SOLDIER *brings files into the office, puts them on the desk and then returns to the outer area.*

SERGEANT. Name.

ERICA. Erica Molnar.

SERGEANT. Molnar, Erica. Sit down.

She sits down as CLARA *reaches out to put the radio on. The* 1ST SOLDIER *goes out.*

LERMONTOV. But perhaps, not now.

He picks up a file and looks through it.

CLARA. It's a very beautiful city. Perhaps that's why they produce such beautiful music.

LERMONTOV. Yes, I think, that that was Offenbach... Where do you come from, comrade?

CLARA. Oh, just a small village, Comrade Lermontov.

LERMONTOV. And have you ever been to Moscow?
Leningrad?

CLARA *shakes her head, smiling. Another* PRISONER *is
brought in by the* 1ST SOLDIER.

Well, they are beautiful cities, too. Even more, perhaps, than
Budapest.

CLARA. Yet how sad that such a place has fallen victim to a
counter-revolutionary coup by reactionary forces.

LERMONTOV. But how fortunate that we have come to its
assistance, to prevent that coup's success.

CLARA. Hear hear.

LERMONTOV *is making to go to the outer area, as the new*
PRISONER *sits.*

LERMONTOV. Comrade, what is your name?

CLARA. Clara Ivanovna.

LERMONTOV. Clara Ivanovna, summon for me, if you will, M
Paloczi.

CLARA *goes to the upper area and calls.*

CLARA. M Paloczi!

The SERGEANT *nods to the* 2ND *and* 3RD SOLDIERS,
who pull PALOCZI *to his feet and push him into the office.*
PALOCZI *wears a long grey overcoat and a slouch hat. He
looks a bit like a gangster. His face is bruised and there are
traces of blood.* CLARA *comes back to her table. The*
SERGEANT *goes out.*

LERMONTOV. Sit.

PALOCZI *sits. The* SOLDIERS *withdraw.* CLARA *picks up
a notepad and pencil.* LERMONTOV *is consulting the file
as he speaks.*

My name is Lieutenant Lermontov. Your name is Miklos
Paloczi. You are twenty-one years old, and a student. You
were arrested at three o'clock this morning, in charge of a
radio transmitter broadcasting illegally from a lodging in the
Corvin Alley district.

PALOCZI *says nothing.*

Yesterday afternoon, you made a broadcast of an apparently
slanderous and provocative character.

He consults a transcript.

In it, you claim that millions of 'landowners and – bishops'
are at large. That 'forty thousand' aristocrats and fascists are
on strike – in C'seppell? This seems unlikely. Could you
explain this to me, please?

PALOCZI *says nothing.*

I'm afraid I don't speak Hungarian. Do you speak Russian?

PALOCZI. I can speak Russian. We can all speak Russian.

LERMONTOV. Good.

PALOCZI. 'Csepel' is pronounced 'Che-*pell*'. It is a large
industrial district to the south of Budapest. It's where a
general strike is going on. Budapest is the city you have just
invaded. It is the capital of Hungary, an independent republic
of ten million people –

LERMONTOV. You're saying that the working class of Csepel,
are all fascists?

Pause. PALOCZI *shakes his head.*

PALOCZI. I was being – irony. Ironical.

LERMONTOV. Comrade, I would seriously advise you not to
be too clever. It was, after all, your government who invited
us to aid you, in your struggle against the White Terror and
reaction.

There is a commotion developing in the outer area. An
OLD WOMAN, *dressed in black, and carrying a string bag,*

is forcing her way in from the street, past the 1ST SOLDIER.
We imagine she is speaking in Hungarian.

OLD WOMAN. Where are my sausages?

1ST SOLDIER. Hey, you can't go in there –

LERMONTOV. We are all well aware of where we are, and
why we're here.

OLD WOMAN (*to* 2ND SOLDIER). Hey, you! I want my
sausages.

   LERMONTOV *aware of the commotion.*

2ND SOLDIER. What's this?

1ST SOLDIER. I don't know, it's some old –

LERMONTOV (*to* PALOCZI). Please excuse me.

   LERMONTOV *and* CLARA *to the doorway between the
   office and the outer area.*

2ND SOLDIER (*taking the* OLD WOMAN*'s arm*). Now,
Granny, you can't come in here.

1ST SOLDIER. She's crazy.

OLD WOMAN. Come on, where are they? Hey?

LERMONTOV (*to* CLARA). Find out what's going on.

CLARA. She wants something I think.

LERMONTOV. That much is clear. Please find out what, and
why.

   CLARA *to the outer area.*

OLD WOMAN. You said that there'd be sausages on Monday.
And some beetroot. I demand my sausages!

   She breaks free.

PALOCZI. I can tell you what she wants.

CLARA (*to* 1ST SOLDIER). What's going on?

1ST SOLDIER. Oh, some old crazy Magyar thinks we're s'posed to feed her.

The OLD WOMAN *is trying to find her sausages. The* 1ST *and* 2ND SOLDIERS *in chase. The* 3RD SOLDIER *nervously keeping other* PRISONERS *covered.*

PALOCZI (*to* LERMONTOV). Till yesterday, this barracks was a distribution centre. For the free food that the peasants brought us from the villages.

2ND SOLDIER (*grabbing the* OLD WOMAN). There – is – no – food. Here – is – the – army. There – is – no – entry – here.

The OLD WOMAN *is at the exit.*

OLD WOMAN. Huh. All the same.

CLARA *laughs. The* 3RD SOLDIER *threatens her. The* OLD WOMAN *spits.*

This time, 'the real revolution'?

The 1ST SOLDIER *manhandles her out.* LERMONTOV *suddenly, to* PALOCZI:

LERMONTOV. Free food?

PALOCZI. That's right.

LERMONTOV. The peasants bring the cities food, for nothing?

PALOCZI. You know, it's no wonder you're all told to stay inside your tanks. Or else you might find out what's happening here.

CLARA *returning.*

LERMONTOV. So why not tell me.

CLARA. It was some mistake. It's sorted out, now, though. She's gone.

CLARA *sits and opens her notebook.*

LERMONTOV (*to* PALOCZI). So why not – tell me?

PALOCZI *is silent. Then a slight nod of his head towards* CLARA, *sitting with her pencil.*

Please leave us.

CLARA. Beg pardon?

LERMONTOV. I said, please leave us for a moment.

CLARA. But I was told / I had to –

LERMONTOV. Can't you hear what I am saying? Do I have to spell it out in semaphore? Please go away.

CLARA *goes. But on her way out, she overhears:*

They're some of them so slow and stupid. Villagers. They've never seen a city. So. Tell me. What has happened here, to make the peasants give away their food for free.

PALOCZI. As opposed to at the point of a bayonet.

Pause.

LERMONTOV. Exactly.

PALOCZI. Oh, well. Why not. What else have I to lose?

He takes off his hat, tosses it on the table, puts his feet up.

A dialectic, Comrade Lermontov. Thesis: 1947. I remember May Day. I was fourteen. Our liberation, from the landowners and counts. A real revolution, bubbling from below. Oh, very rushed and slapdash, but – still, real. And ours.

And then, antithesis, we found out the revolution wasn't ours, but yours. Your language and your culture papered over ours. And, if I may say so, your methods of control. And people felt betrayed. We felt betrayed.

LERMONTOV. And, synthesis?

PALOCZI. Okay. Last week. A meeting. In a village. All talk, and shouting, bickering and chaos; someone trying to organise a march on Budapest, someone else attempting to brew up tea on the bars of an electric fire. And a group of stolid peasants in some corner, furrowed brows, attempting to elect something or other; and they apologised, to me,

I can't think why, that it was all taking such a time. You see, they hadn't actually elected anything before. And I thought, glory be. This time: a real revolution. Ours.

LERMONTOV. But Communists were murdered.

PALOCZI. Were they?

LERMONTOV. Criminals and killers were set loose. Ordinary Communists, good Communists were lynched. Their hearts cut out.

PALOCZI. Maybe.

LERMONTOV. These things occurred.

Pause. PALOCZI *puts his feet down.*

PALOCZI. Look. A revolution is a festival. Lenin said that, I was surprised to learn. And the thing about a festival is that it's very tricky to control. We have been drunk this last few weeks. For most of us, exhilaration. But for some, revenge. Mistakes get made. But the point is, that some crazy drunk stopped the collectivisation of the farms. And compulsory deliveries of food. And so the peasants loaded up their carts with everything that they could spare, and brought it here, and gave it to the people. Because, at last, they trusted them.

You know, I imagine, comrade, the October revolution was very much a festival.

LERMONTOV. You know, I think you're right.

PALOCZI. About 1917?

LERMONTOV. I think there's been an error.

PALOCZI. Or what's happening here?

LERMONTOV. I think you're the wrong man. You are not Miklos Paloczi.

PALOCZI. Eh?

LERMONTOV. I think it's a mistake, and you should go.

He's marking the file. Quickly:

Go now. Go anywhere. You can still get to the border. Now!

PALOCZI *stands, his face is white.*

PALOCZI. Why, Comrade Lermontov?

LERMONTOV (*deliberately*). Because – I am of the view – that revolutions should correct mistakes. If they are not to lose people's trust. And so – I'm trusting you. And yes, because I think it's happening here.

Pause.

The border! Now!

PALOCZI (*blurted*). Will I get five yards beyond that door?

LERMONTOV. Maybe. Who knows?

PALOCZI. Give me your revolver.

LERMONTOV. You know I can't do that.

PALOCZI. I won't get far without it.

LERMONTOV. I can't go that far.

Slight pause. LERMONTOV *goes to the box of confiscated weapons, and finds a grenade. He hands it to* PALOCZI.

Take that. It is – a sort of hand grenade.

PALOCZI *grins, puts his hat on, turns to go.*

How long?

PALOCZI. How – what?

LERMONTOV. For how long, do you think, will peasants give their food away? A month? A year? For ever?

Pause.

PALOCZI. Maybe. Who knows.

He looks at the grenade and smiles.

It's one of ours.

LERMONTOV *nods to the side door, and* PALOCZI *slips out.* LERMONTOV *makes another note on* PALOCZI'*s file. There is a burst of gunfire from offstage.* LERMONTOV *looks towards it. Then, quickly, to the outer area:*

LERMONTOV. Next!

1ST SOLDIER (*to* ERICA). Stand up!

2ND SOLDIER. Quickly!

ERICA *stands. The* 1ST *and* 2ND SOLDIERS *jab and shove her into the office.*

LERMONTOV. Right. And you are…

ERICA. Erica Molnar.

A shout from outside.

VOICE. Help! Help me, please…

LERMONTOV. What's that?

A YOUNG SOLDIER *rushes into the outer area. He is badly burnt. His hands in front of his face, his uniform ripped and charred. The other* SOLDIERS *rush to his aid, one turning back to cover any other* PRISONERS. CLARA *appears.*

YOUNG SOLDIER. Oh, Holy Mother, help me.

LERMONTOV *towards the upper area, drawing a revolver.*

1ST SOLDIER (*to* 2ND SOLDIER). A doctor, get a doctor, quick.

CLARA *to the* YOUNG SOLDIER *as the* 2ND SOLDIER *runs out.*

YOUNG SOLDIER. Oh, no. God have mercy on me. Help me. Please.

The 1ST SOLDIER *helps the* YOUNG SOLDIER *out. We still hear him crying.* CLARA *goes into the office.*

CLARA. It's terrible. A barricade. And no one there. He stopped and opened up his tank, to take a look… They think, it was a young man with a hand grenade…

Pause. CLARA *is surprised to see* ERICA.

Where is – Where's the other one?

LERMONTOV. He wasn't who we thought he was. It was a mix-up. Such things happen. All the time.

CLARA. There was some shooting, out there. Just before...

LERMONTOV. Apparently, they missed.

He strides out quickly. CLARA *looks at* ERICA.

CHORUS. November 1956. At the request of the Hungarian workers and peasants, the Soviet Army extends temporary help to the Hungarian government and people in overcoming counter-revolution and restoring order.

The Soviet Union invades Hungary.

August 1961. In the face of the aggression of West Germany and its imperialist allies, an anti-fascist protection barrier has been erected in Berlin, to ensure the territorial integrity of the German Democratic Republic.

The East Germans build a wall dividing Berlin.

August 1968. To confront a reactionary assault upon the foundations of the Czechoslovak Socialist Republic, the government calls on the friendly countries of the socialist bloc for fraternal assistance.

Moscow. Red Square.

Scene Two

Red Square, Moscow. August 1968. A couple of POLICEMEN, *and maybe a couple of* CIVILIANS, *who might also be* POLICEMEN. *Enter a rather dusty-looking, middle-aged academic, called* PUGACHEV, *and* LERMONTOV.

PUGACHEV. Comrade Lermontov.

LERMONTOV. Comrade Pugachev.

PUGACHEV. Why are we here?

LERMONTOV. Leonid Sergeyevich, doctor of philology, candidate member, the Academy of Sciences.

PUGACHEV (*not sure of the point*). Pavel Mikhailovich, translator, the Institute of International Cultural Exchange. What is going on?

LERMONTOV (*striding off*). We're going on a scientific expedition.

PUGACHEV (*following, unhappily*). In Red Square?

LERMONTOV. That's right. Because this is where it happened.

PUGACHEV (*still unhappy*). What happened?

LERMONTOV. This is the position of the pram, wheeled by the poetess. Who meets the other seven, who have converged on the square from different directions, choosing this spot because it's not near a traffic lane.

PUGACHEV. I see.

LERMONTOV. The poetess reaches under the mattress of the pram – under her baby – and produces banners. One bears the ancient Polish slogan: 'For your freedom – and for ours.'

PUGACHEV (*making to go*). Yes, fine, Pavel –

LERMONTOV. And if you take another step, I will shout out what the other banner said.

PUGACHEV *stops*.

PUGACHEV. All right. Just be quick.

LERMONTOV. They sit here, on the ground. A whistle blows. KGB men, in civilian clothes, rush from all sides.

PUGACHEV (*looking round warily*). Yes, they do that.

LERMONTOV. As they run, they shout: 'Look at those Jews and traitors!'

PUGACHEV. And that too.

LERMONTOV. The art historian is here, when they hit him in the face and break his teeth. The physicist is here, when they hit him with a heavy suitcase. The cars arrived there, there and there, and take the six away. The mother and her baby sit here for ten minutes, when they come and take her too. They beat her in the car. The other slogan reads: 'Hands off Czechoslovakia.'

Pause.

That's the country we have just invaded.

PUGACHEV. That's the country into which we were just invited.

LERMONTOV. What?

PUGACHEV. Yes, of course I heard about it. There was a meeting at the university, to condemn the hooligans.

LERMONTOV. I am assembling a petition, to request their release.

PUGACHEV. Look, Pavel, I'm sure it's all a regrettable mistake –

LERMONTOV. I remember Hungary. I was there. That, too, was 'a regrettable mistake'. And yet, here it is, happening again.

Pause.

PUGACHEV. Look, can we go now, please, Pavel?

LERMONTOV. My petition reads –

PUGACHEV. I'm afraid my memories are less – dramatic.

LERMONTOV. To the Procurator General, the Union / of
    Soviet –

PUGACHEV. I just remember living with three other families
    in a freezing room divided by old sheets hung from the
    ceiling. And being hungry from the age of eight to the age of
    seventeen.

LERMONTOV. And now you are a comfortable professor. And
    you want to stay that way.

PUGACHEV. Look, of course I'm on their side. But a
    demonstration, seen by no one. Lasting twenty seconds.

    That is just – ridiculous.

    I'm so sorry, Pavel Mikhailovich.

    PUGACHEV *exits*. LERMONTOV *stays where he is, as
    another man*, SKURATOV, *enters*.

Scene Three

*An office in Moscow, October 1968. A desk, two chairs, a waste-
paper basket.* SKURATOV *has a file*.

SKURATOV. Comrade Lermontov. How good of you to drop
    by. Please do sit down. My name is Skuratov.

    He gestures to LERMONTOV *to sit*.

    Perhaps you can guess the reason for our chat?

    LERMONTOV *sits*. SKURATOV *puts a document in front
    of* LERMONTOV *and sits as well*.

    Perhaps you would explain this document to me.

    LERMONTOV *looks at it*.

LERMONTOV. It's a petition to the Procurator General. About
    seven people who were / arrested –

SKURATOV. So I think that's probably the answer.

LERMONTOV. In other words, a completely legal document –

SKURATOV. Which you drew up and then released to foreign correspondents.

LERMONTOV. I sent it to *Isvestia*. They didn't print it.

SKURATOV. No, well, a paper can't print everything. And so, instead, you send it to the *New York Times*. So they could try to beam it back, on shortwave radio.

LERMONTOV. That was never my intention.

SKURATOV. No? Read this.

He shows another piece of paper to LERMONTOV, *who starts to read it to himself.*

Out loud.

LERMONTOV. 'All week the raucous and corrupt Voice of America has been shrieking hoarsely. True to its creed of provocation, this CIA-backed organ of war criminals and émigrés have cynically sought to elevate' – *has* cynically sought – 'a gang of ne'er-do-wells and hooligans to the status of "Defenders of the People". Sadly, in their unsavoury campaign of falsehood, the imperialists have secured a willing ally.'

Seeing what's next, he stops. SKURATOV *takes the paper back.*

SKURATOV. 'In the shape of one PM Lermontov. The Soviet people will not stoop to parley words with such haughty renegades.' Now, this *was* accepted by *Isvestia*.

LERMONTOV. I didn't see it.

SKURATOV. No one has seen it. It's not being published till tomorrow.

Slight pause.

The author, CI Kaminskaya, goes on – will go on – to call upon the office of the Procurator to bring the full force of the law to bear upon such arrogant and childish slanderers. Are you aware of the provisions of Article 70 of the Criminal Code of the RSFSR?

LERMONTOV. I am aware that Article 125 of the Constitution of the USSR guarantees freedom of speech, assembly, demonstration –

SKURATOV. And its related penalties?

Slight pause.

LERMONTOV. What do you want of me?

SKURATOV. I want you to write an article.

LERMONTOV. What, for / *Isvestia.*

SKURATOV. *Isvestia.*

LERMONTOV. About?

SKURATOV. Your change of mind.

LERMONTOV. I haven't had a change of mind.

SKURATOV. Well, then, your change of heart.

He takes a document from his file and shows it to
LERMONTOV.

I've no doubt you'll have views about the grammar.

As LERMONTOV *reads:*

Now, look, old chap. This country nursed you, raised you, taught you. And now you turn on us.

Pause.

As CI Kaminskaya stresses, you were an army officer for seven years. You served in Hungary.

LERMONTOV. And yet, here I am. An agent of US imperialism.

SKURATOV. What?

LERMONTOV. And a fascist, naturally.

SKURATOV. You don't mean that.

LERMONTOV. No, of course I don't mean that.

SKURATOV. Then why…?

LERMONTOV. I was being…

He is surprised by what he is about to say.

It was irony.

Slight pause. LERMONTOV *screws up the article and throws it on the floor.* SKURATOV *stands, closing the file.*

SKURATOV. Oh, irony. Of course. How stupid of me, not to pick it up. But then I'd imagine you think everyone is pretty dull and stupid, in comparison with you.

LERMONTOV. I didn't say that.

SKURATOV. Didn't even think it, I imagine. But I suspect it's what you feel.

He picks up the article, smooths it out, and puts it in the file.

LERMONTOV. You didn't seriously think that I'd agree to this.

SKURATOV. No. But now you will think seriously. About your actions. And their consequences. Don't say I didn't warn you.

He goes out. Pause. LERMONTOV *stands. He changes into a grey quilted prison jacket, as the Soviet national anthem is played, tinnily, through loudspeakers, and the next scene emerges.* PUGACHEV *appears.*

PUGACHEV. The Criminal Code of the Russian Soviet Federative Socialist Republic.

SKURATOV. Article 70.

PUGACHEV. 'Agitation or propaganda carried on for the purpose of subverting or weakening Soviet power, or of circulating for the same purpose slanderous fabrications which defame the Soviet state and social system, shall be punished by deprivation of freedom for a term of six months to seven years.'

Scene Four

*The Hospital Camp in Dubrovlag camp complex in Mordovia.
Autumn 1971. Evening. There could be* GUARDS *in
watchtowers. A row of naked light bulbs.*

A young man called KOROLENKO, *in a grey quilted jacket,
sits on a bench outside a guardhouse.* LERMONTOV *sits with
him. In front of them, on the ground, a stretcher, on which lies a*
PRISONER *under a rough blanket.*

KOROLENKO. 1971. Dubrovlag. Oak Forest Camp. Garden of
Eden.

He looks at LERMONTOV, *who says nothing.*

Hey. Adam and Eve. First Communists. Know why?

LERMONTOV *looks at* KOROLENKO.

No clothes, one apple between them, and they thought they
were in paradise.

KOROLENKO *laughs.* LERMONTOV *a slight smile.*

All right. D'you know what's similar, between the Garden of
Eden and the Great Soviet Socialist Democracy?

LERMONTOV. No, tell me.

KOROLENKO. God creates Eve, says to Adam, go on, pick a
woman.

LERMONTOV (*smiles, turning away*). Mm.

KOROLENKO. Okay. Three zeks, on their way here, on the
train, telling each other what they're in for. First one: 'I
spoke ill of Comrade Popov.' Second: 'I spoke well of
Comrade Popov.' Third one: 'I *am…*'

LERMONTOV (*laughs*). '…Comrade Popov.'

KOROLENKO. So. What you in for?

LERMONTOV. Me? I spoke to the wrong people.

KOROLENKO. Oh, ar? Different with me. I spoke to the right people.

LERMONTOV. What d'you mean?

An OFFICER *enters briskly.* KOROLENKO *leaps to his feet,* LERMONTOV *stands more formally.*

KOROLENKO. Please, sir. Please, comrade sir.

OFFICER. Yes, what?

KOROLENKO. Please, comrade sir. We need an escort. To take this patient back to the ward, sir.

OFFICER. Patient?

KOROLENKO. Yes, sir. He's had an operation. The anaesthetic will be wearing off.

OFFICER. An operation? Anaesthetic? What d'you think I am? A doctor?

KOROLENKO. No, sir.

OFFICER. Well, then. There you are.

He strides out. KOROLENKO *and* LERMONTOV *sit.*

KOROLENKO. Well, it all started, something of a cock-up, really. See, I was working in a coal mine, in Donetsk, you know it?

LERMONTOV. Well, I've heard of it.

KOROLENKO. And there were all kinds of problems. Safety regulations weren't being met. Dangerous build-ups of methane gas. And we were being forced to work Red Saturdays.

Well, this didn't seem quite fair to me.

So I started writing letters. I wrote to Comrade General Secretary Brezhnev, and to Comrade Premier Kosygin. And to many other comrades. But, apparently, these comrades, these great men, are of a highly nervous and susceptible disposition, because, low 'n' behold, I get hauled up in court, accused of causing 'em considerable agitation. And apparently, I found, there is this cunning little law...

But I've only three weeks left. And then I'm free. Look on the bright side, eh?

Pause.

So, who d'you talk to, then?

LERMONTOV. I'm sorry?

KOROLENKO. Said, you talked to the wrong people.

A female DOCTOR, *in civilian clothes, enters briskly.* KOROLENKO *leaps up.* LERMONTOV *follows.*

Ah, doctor. Comrade doctor.

The DOCTOR *carries on.*

Comrade doctor!

The DOCTOR *turns.*

DOCTOR. Yes?

KOROLENKO. We are the stretcher party, comrade doctor. We need an escort, for this prisoner. To return him to his ward.

Slight pause.

DOCTOR. Am I a doctor?

KOROLENKO. Yes?

DOCTOR. Am I an escort?

KOROLENKO. No?

DOCTOR. Do you need a doctor, or an escort?

KOROLENKO. Well –

The DOCTOR *goes quickly out. The* PRISONER *moves slightly.*

He's coming round! He definitely moved!

Silence.

LERMONTOV. What was his operation?

KOROLENKO. Oh, an ironmonger's job.

LERMONTOV. I'm sorry?

KOROLENKO. Kettle spout. Spoon handle. Bits of barbed wire. Stuff like that.

He sits. LERMONTOV *sits. Pause.*

So what d'you do, before?

LERMONTOV. I was a translator.

KOROLENKO. Ah. A 'destabilising element'. A 'slavish imitator of the West'. If not a 'parasitic hooligan'.

LERMONTOV. Exactly.

KOROLENKO. So are you writing in here, then? Things for the West, in here?

LERMONTOV *says nothing.*

I sometimes think, if people only knew…

Pause.

LERMONTOV. Then what?

KOROLENKO. It wouldn't happen.

LERMONTOV. No?

Pause.

Look, I have a friend. In Moscow. And he's a university professor: and he has most of what our society can offer; a good job, good apartment, foreign travel, even, sometimes, to the West… And he knows. Of course he knows.

KOROLENKO. Think so?

LERMONTOV. And I think also of a writer whom I don't know personally and I doubt if I ever shall. Called CI Kaminskaya, who writes articles in *Isvestia*. And who once wrote an article on me. An extraordinary polemic. 'Renegade,

hooligan.' 'Misfit, slanderer.' And my fear is that CI
Kaminskaya really is the trumpet of this people. That the dull
and stupid hatred she expresses really is the general will.

KOROLENKO. Really? Even here?

LERMONTOV. My friend, apparently, they say, that somewhere
on the further reaches of this wilderness of camps, there is a
prisoner who fought at Kronstadt. Who has been here ever
since the sailors' rising was put down by Trotsky, fifty years
ago. And that old man has seen Utopia's refuse pile up all
around him, all those years: all those generations of class
enemies, class traitors, ists and iks and ites: adventurists,
capitulationists, and schizophrenics; Trotskyites and
Titoites... Until the pile of shit and sewerage, the effluent of
paradise, rose up to drown the spires and steeples of the
city... And through all of them this old man passes, like a
ghost, our Holy Fool. And having seen it all, says nothing.

Pause.

KOROLENKO. So you are writing then.

Writing things like that down, for the West.

Pause.

I'm out in three weeks, me.

Pause.

LERMONTOV. What is your name?

KOROLENKO. I'm Anatoly Korolenko.

LERMONTOV. From Donetsk.

KOROLENKO. Well, not originally. Originally, I'm from a
grubby little peasant village. Guess what, I've never been to
Moscow.

Slight pause.

Look at it this way. I grass on you, you get a few more years.
I take your writing and it's published in the West, you get a
few more years.

What have you got to lose?

Pause.

LERMONTOV. How can a human being not trust someone?

KOROLENKO. That's the spirit.

Pause. A CHIEF OFFICER *enters.* KOROLENKO *leaps to his feet.* LERMONTOV *follows, quicker.*

Chief officer! Chief comrade officer! Two prisoners require an escort to transport this prisoner to his ward, comrade chief officer chief sir.

Pause.

CHIEF OFFICER. Is this – Are you complaining?

KOROLENKO. No, sir!

CHIEF OFFICER. Do you want the cooler?

KOROLENKO. No, sir!

Slight pause.

CHIEF OFFICER. Right.

The CHIEF OFFICER *goes out. The two men remain to attention.*

KOROLENKO. I think you're wrong. I think there's millions out there. Renegades and misfits. If they only knew.

Two clangs – a hammer on a rail. Slight pause. Two more. KOROLENKO *breaks his stance.*

(*Outraged.*) And now it's Lights Out. *Lights Out.* We're still here.

He throws himself on the bench. The PRISONER *coming round.*

PRISONER. Uh? What?

KOROLENKO. So you write it down, and I take it to your friend.

LERMONTOV *stands.* GUARDS *enter with the shabby suit he wore on the Glienicke Bridge. He changes, as:*

CHORUS. 1972. The Strategic Arms Limitation Agreement signals the commencement of a positive period of mutual understanding between the United States of America and the peace-loving peoples of the Union of Soviet Socialist Republics.

PUGACHEV *enters from one direction, and* KOROLENKO *from another. As they pass,* KOROLENKO *hands a document to* PUGACHEV. *They both go out. As:*

AMANDA. 1973. Amanda leaves Socialist Vanguard.

MARTIN. 1974. Martin is expelled from Socialist Vanguard.

MARTIN. 1975. Martin attends a party in North London.

CHORUS. Britain votes two to one to stay in the European Common Market.

1977. The National Front gains nearly a quarter of a million votes in the local elections.

AMANDA. 1978. Amanda and her daughter Tanya attend an Anti-Nazi Carnival in Victoria Park, East London.

She sees JAMES, *who holds up a copy of* The Times.

JAMES. 'Martin Glass: A change of mind.' *The Times*.

AMANDA. 'My change of heart.' The *Guardian*.

JAMES. The Oxford Union. Panorama. Any Questions. 'I didn't leave the Left –

AMANDA *and* JAMES. – it left me.'

JAMES. I told you. Just on holiday.

Enter MARTIN. *During this*, JEREMY, PALOCZI *and* LERMONTOV *appear.*

MARTIN. I was attracted to the revolutionary Left by the heroism of those fighting for liberty and equality. Until I realised that, in the real world, liberty and equality are contradictory. That men and women are only really equal in the prison or the graveyard. And that all attempts to force them to be equal – every increase in the power of the state – leads ultimately to the concentration camp.

LERMONTOV *faces* PALOCZI. MARTIN *faces* JEREMY.

JEREMY. Then, welcome.

Part Three

I'm not sure, you see, that the masses really *want* personal liberty. In fact, I've a strong feeling that, at heart, they are afraid of the challenge and responsibility it implies. They like being governed and told what to do. Liberty is, and always has been, an intellectual concept of the minority... It is the elite who must reawaken to the meaning of liberty, and fight for it, because it is the elite of the West who are going to win this battle...

> Boris Bajanov (former secretary to Stalin),
> *Sunday Telegraph*, 3 October 1976

If one were to probe into the hearts of many potential and actual Tory supporters – and others besides – one might well discover that what worries them most about contemporary Britain was not so much the lack of freedom as its excessive abundance; not so much the threat of dictatorship as the reality of something unpleasantly close to chaos... and for Mrs Thatcher to tell a party indignant at the collapse of all forms of authority, and longing for the smack of Firm Government, that the country is suffering from a lack of liberty makes her seem out of touch with reality...

> Peregrine Worsthorne, *Conservative Essays*, 1978

We are reaping what was sown in the sixties. The fashionable theories and permissive claptrap set the set for a society in which the old virtues of discipline and self-restraint were denigrated.

> Margaret Thatcher, 27 March 1982

Scene One

Heathrow Airport. Late 1978. PALOCZI *quickly leads in* LERMONTOV, *followed by a large gaggle of* REPORTERS *and* CAMERAMEN. *The* REPORTERS *shriek questions. The* CAMERAMEN *flash away.*

LERMONTOV *looks totally bewildered, as* PALOCZI *leads him towards a microphone. All this very fast:*

REPORTERS (*variously*). When were you released, Mr Lermontov?

When did they tell you?

Please look over here, Mr Lermontov.

What does it feel like, to be in the West?

How long ago did you know?

Mr Lermontov, just turn your head, please –

What do you feel about being exchanged for a Russian spy?

PALOCZI. Please, please, ladies and gentlemen...

REPORTERS. Did they tell you in advance?

Did you want to be exiled to the West?

Just look this way, Mr Lermontov –

Do you have any family left in Russia?

Where are you staying in England, Mr Lermontov?

PALOCZI *and* LERMONTOV *are at the microphone. Discreetly,* PALOCZI *hands* LERMONTOV *cards.*

Which hotel are you staying at?

How long will you be staying there?

Do you have any immediate plans?

Why did you choose to come to England?

Here, please, Mr Lermontov –

When were you told about your release?

PALOCZI. Mr Lermontov is very tired. He will make a short statement.

LERMONTOV (*reading the cards in English, in his Russian accent*). I have come here, as a witness, from a – totally?

PALOCZI. Totalitarian.

LERMONTOV. – totalitarian society, to a free one. I come with joy, but also with a warning. That unless you guard your freedom, from the forces which now threaten it, from without and from within, you may end up living in a country like my country. Thank you.

PALOCZI *quickly shepherds* LERMONTOV *out*.

REPORTERS. What do you mean by 'totalitarian society'?

What threat do you refer to?

Do you think Britain is like Russia?

What things frighten you about Britain?

Can you expand on what you've said?

Scene Two

December 1978. A suite in a hotel in Kensington. Hightech, tubular design. JEREMY *is reading newspapers.* PALOCZI *is on the telephone.*

JEREMY (*reading from a newspaper*). The University of Loughborough is planning to spend twenty thousand pounds researching something they describe as 'pinball art'.

PALOCZI. What, actually in the lobby?

JEREMY. And apparently, it's been proposed that the Inner London Education Authority provide free crèche facilities for schoolgirl mothers. As of 'right'.

PALOCZI. No, they must ring.

JEREMY. Free in the sense of 'on the rates', of course.

PALOCZI. No, Mr Lermontov is already booked for interview. *The Sunday Times*. Exclusively.

JEREMY. Sometimes I think they print these things, deliberately, just to outrage me.

A knock at the door. JEREMY *goes to answer it.*

PALOCZI. And now, please hold all calls.

He puts the phone down as JEREMY *admits* MARTIN, *who looks scruffy for the environment.*

JEREMY. Martin.

MARTIN. They wouldn't let me in.

PALOCZI *is coming over to* MARTIN *and* JEREMY.

JEREMY. Well, it's a very superior establishment.

MARTIN. What do you mean?

PALOCZI. Perhaps Professor Crowther is referring to the scarf.

MARTIN. Oh, so there's a dress code?

PALOCZI (*his hand out*). I'm Miklos Paloczi.

JEREMY. Founder of the Free Pavel Lermontov Campaign.

Enter LERMONTOV *from the bedroom.*

LERMONTOV. Forgive me, I have overslept. The *towels*.

PALOCZI. Pavel.

MARTIN *and* JEREMY *to their feet.*

LERMONTOV. Now, these are –

PALOCZI. Now, Pavel, meet –

LERMONTOV. Professor Crowther?

JEREMY. Jeremy.

He shakes LERMONTOV*'s hand.*

LERMONTOV. I understand from Miklos I have much to thank you for.

JEREMY *gives a demurring gesture.*

Were all those calls for me?

PALOCZI. Yes. Do you want to hear about them?

LERMONTOV *sits.*

LERMONTOV. Please. It's such a...

(*To* PALOCZI, *in 'Russian'.*) New thing?

PALOCZI. Novelty.

Reading from his notebook:

The BBC World Service people rang. They want you for an interview. They tried to fob us off with a man called Andreyushkin, but I told them where they could put that. They're calling back.

MARTIN. What's wrong with Andreyushkin?

PALOCZI. Soft.

MARTIN. On what?

PALOCZI. You name it. Arms control. Detente. Very weak on Vietnam.

LERMONTOV. Aha.

PALOCZI. And then there were lots of papers, but I said *The Sunday Times*... And various cranks and crazies whom you needn't bother with.

MARTIN. I'm sorry, cranks and crazies?

A difficult pause.

LERMONTOV (*to* JEREMY). Well, now. Miklos informs me
you are interviewing me.

MARTIN. In fact, it's me.

LERMONTOV. *The Sunday Times*.

PALOCZI. Correct.

LERMONTOV (*to* MARTIN). And you, a former Trotskyist?
Is that unusual?

PALOCZI. Um…

Slight pause.

JEREMY. Well, Martin / obviously –

LERMONTOV. Please. After all, you could say, we are both
defectors.

MARTIN. All right. Look. I became a revolutionary socialist to
set the people free from state authority. Until I realised that
authority and power was what the left was all about.

JEREMY (*to* LERMONTOV). In your country and in ours.

MARTIN. I'm still with the malcontents and the subversives.
I don't think I've changed.

PALOCZI. But do you think they really want it? Freedom?

MARTIN. Who?

PALOCZI. 'The people.'

MARTIN. Well, I think / that –

PALOCZI. Because, you see, I detect complete contentment
with the national lot. The supine masses, slumped before the
television, or down the pub, cashing their giro cheques, with
their darts and dogs and pinball.

MARTIN. What's wrong with pinball?

PALOCZI. And of course, in power, union bully boys.
Blockheads in big boots. And where we come from,
apparatchiks and commissars. And with that, too, the masses,
blissfully content.

MARTIN. Oh, do you think so? I think, if you really set the people free, from the union bosses and the state, you'd be amazed how many Michelangelos could bloom.

PALOCZI (*with a dismissive smile*). Michelangelos?

JEREMY (*with a glance at his watch*). Now, in fact, the table's booked for / half-past –

MARTIN *a demurring gesture. The phone rings.*

PALOCZI (*answering phone*). And I did say no calls. Hallo?

LERMONTOV. And may I ask, when you change your political opinion, is there reaction from your former comrades?

PALOCZI (*into phone*). Oh, yes, of course.

JEREMY. Yes, Martin was subject to considerable abuse. 'Traitor. Judas.'

MARTIN. 'Turncoat.'

LERMONTOV (*to* PALOCZI). 'Turncoat'?

PALOCZI (*to* LERMONTOV). Renegade.

(*Into phone.*) Certainly.

LERMONTOV. Ah. CI Kaminskaya.

PALOCZI (*into phone*). Yes, in fact, he's here…

MARTIN. But, obviously, nothing to compare…

LERMONTOV. But, still…

PALOCZI (*into phone*). Of course. Look, let me call you back.

He puts the phone down.

(*To* LERMONTOV.) There is a body, called the Centre for the National Interest. They want to give you an award. A big ceremony in London. That was the chairman. He's a former member of the government, now the Provost of a Cambridge College.

Slight pause.

LERMONTOV. Then, of course. I'd be most privileged.

PALOCZI. No doubt you'll have to make a speech.

LERMONTOV. No doubt you'll write it for me.

PALOCZI. If you like.

Slight pause.

LERMONTOV. And now, with my fellow defector, to lunch?

PALOCZI. Of course.

PALOCZI *and* LERMONTOV *go out.* MARTIN *lingering.*

MARTIN. Jeremy.

JEREMY. Yes, what?

MARTIN. Who is that man?

JEREMY. Miklos Paloczi. Chatham House.

MARTIN. I mean, *who* is he? What's he doing?

JEREMY. Well, what he's done is to spend eight years
    campaigning for our friend to be / released –

MARTIN. 'The supine mass.' 'Weak on Vietnam.'

JEREMY. Yes, I'd imagine that means –

MARTIN. Do you think the US should have been in Vietnam?

JEREMY. I think so, yes. Don't you?

MARTIN. I'm a libertarian. I distrust governments. The people
    who fight wars.

PALOCZI *re-enters.*

JEREMY. Well, on resisting military might, Paloczi does have
    impeccable credentials. In fact you could say, that unlike me,
    he left Hungary, over the Party.

MARTIN. And what in God's name is 'the Centre for the
    National Interest'?

JEREMY. It's a pressure group. I'm on its council.

MARTIN. And this Provost?

JEREMY. Sir Hugh Trelawney. Martin –

MARTIN. Hugh Trelawney.

PALOCZI. A tragic story, in a way. Poor bloke got kicked upstairs. There was some, well, unpleasantness, surrounding the enactment of some Act of Parliament.

MARTIN. The Housing Bill.

JEREMY *taking off his tie*.

JEREMY. But more importantly, he has disagreements about the direction of the Party.

MARTIN. The Conservative Party?

JEREMY. Yes.

PALOCZI. Hence his issuing an invitation to his college.

MARTIN. What, to Lermontov?

PALOCZI. No. You.

JEREMY *hands his tie to* MARTIN.

CHORUS, *including a* YOUNG WOMAN *with pink hair:*

CHORUS. September 1978: Sixty thousand Ford workers reject the government's five-per-cent pay limit and go on strike.

Smash the wage freeze!

January 1979: Lorry drivers go on strike, closing thousands of petrol stations and oil refineries.

What do we want?

Ten per cent!

When do we want it?

Now!

January 1979. A Day of Action by public-sector workers –

many black

largely women

– is the largest labour stoppage since the General Strike.

Prime Minister Callaghan returns from an international summit in the Caribbean and denies that there is mounting chaos.

Or, as *The Sun* headline puts it:

'Crisis, what crisis?'

Scene Three

The Provost's rooms, a Cambridge College, January 1979. A roaring fire. JEREMY *has just introduced* MARTIN *to the College Provost,* SIR HUGH TRELAWNEY. *Decanters on tables.*

TRELAWNEY. Now, Mr Glass?

MARTIN. That's right.

JEREMY. Martin, meet Sir Hugh Trelawney.

MARTIN. How do you do?

TRELAWNEY. Welcome to Simeon. Delighted you could make it. Filthy weather.

MARTIN. Not at all.

Slight pause.

TRELAWNEY. I read with interest your piece on Lermontov, where was it?

MARTIN. *Sunday Times*.

TRELAWNEY. Great interest.

Slight pause.

JEREMY. Um, Martin. Hugh was saying –

TRELAWNEY. Hugh will say.

He gestures MARTIN *to sit.* MARTIN *perches on the edge of a sofa.*

In fact, Hugh thought of offering you a job, with our little Institute.

MARTIN. What kind of job?

TRELAWNEY. We had in mind, the preparation of a kind of, manifesto.

MARTIN. For?

TRELAWNEY. To outline what, in our view, the priorities of the next government should be.

MARTIN. Which might represent a change of strategy?

TRELAWLEY. Perspective.

MARTIN. With, perhaps, you back among the leadership?

TRELAWNEY. Come come.

JEREMY. Hugh also thought you might make a contribution to proceedings at the ceremony.

Pause.

MARTIN. You first?

TRELAWNEY. It's an outworn phrase, of course, but the next election will, in my view, be the most important since the war. The showdown, if you like. The polity a pyramid, the electorate a silver ball, perched on the top, unsteady, could roll either way.

MARTIN. A pyramid has several sides.

TRELAWNEY. Of course. And the side that you are on – the side that you are *now* on – is very clear. Unless we want to end up in the Gulag, stop the clicking ratchet of state power.

MARTIN. That's right.

TRELAWNEY. Health warnings off the packets, nanny off our backs. Free, adult men and women in a free, grown-up society.

MARTIN. Correct.

TRELAWNEY. And if people want to buy pornography or drugs, and if they're offered on the market at a price they are prepared to pay, then nobody, and least of all the state, should interfere.

MARTIN. I'm glad that you agree.

TRELAWNEY. I think – about your article – the word I used was 'interesting'.

Pause.

MARTIN (*with a glance at* JEREMY). Go on.

TRELAWNEY. Well, the fact is, on a cursory inspection of your output, I have noticed that the word 'right' – as in 'human right' – has graced your columns, oh, a hundred times. But I've only seen the word 'duty' once.

MARTIN. What's wrong with human rights?

TRELAWNEY. That so often they're not balanced by a corresponding consciousness of obligation.

MARTIN. Well, I'm not that interested in duty.

TRELAWNEY. While I am very interested in what happens in its absence.

MARTIN. Well?

TRELAWNEY. The triumph of the spoiled, the petulant, the infantile. The idea that every appetite is an entitlement. Society an open mouth, the state a ladle. Students, strikers: 'I want always gets.' A debility which it is now our party's task to purge.

MARTIN. What antidote do you prescribe?

TRELAWNEY. Well, in a word: Authority.

Pause.

MARTIN. Well, I'm sorry. But I think I've spent too long believing that the choir of humankind sounds best in unison. I'm really very sorry.

TRELAWNEY. Not unison – so much as harmony.

MARTIN is about to say something, but TRELAWNEY *goes straight on.*

Look, I do – I think I understand. How hard it is.

MARTIN. How hard what is?

TRELAWNEY. What you have had to do. Remake your life. To spend its second half reneging on its first.

MARTIN. Well, I wouldn't say, / entirely –

TRELAWNEY. And of course, I understand, old loyalties.

MARTIN. That wasn't what I said.

TRELAWNEY. That, I completely understand.

MARTIN. Please don't. Call my commitment into question. I know all about commitment. I once had a friend, for instance, committed to assassinating you.

Pause.

TRELAWNEY. Precisely.

MARTIN (*to* JEREMY). Do you agree with this?

JEREMY. With what?

MARTIN. 'Duty.' 'Authority.'

JEREMY. Yes, I think so.

MARTIN. 'I'm with the malcontents, I haven't changed'?

JEREMY. Well, that does depend, of course, on which malcontents you mean.

MARTIN. There's no 'of course' about it, Jeremy.

TRELAWNEY. Look. We all agree about the monolithic, bloated state, failing to run the steelworks or the schools.

We're all for the brisk chill wind of competition. That's the means. But it's not the end. That's something very different.

MARTIN. And what's that?

TRELAWNEY. Oh, a loyalty to something greater than the self. Those things we owe it to the dead to pass on to the yet unborn.

MARTIN. What, the mystic oneness of our island race? 'I Vow to Thee, My Country'? Send the darkies home?

TRELAWNEY. Now, please.

Slight pause.

MARTIN. Look. I shouldn't be here. I should go.

TREWLANEY. Of course. If you're...

MARTIN. I'm sorry to miss dinner.

He goes out.

JEREMY. I'm sorry.

TRELAWNEY. It's the hardest place. The pit stop on the road to Damascus. When you don't know if you're going forward or still looking back.

JEREMY. I'm afraid he won't get very far. It's snowing, and of course the bloody gritters are on strike. The latest is apparently the gravediggers.

TRELAWNEY. Ah, yes.

Re-enter MARTIN *with his coat.*

JEREMY. So you drive because there are no trains, you crash because the roads are ice, and if you're killed you lie unburied.

TRELAWNEY (*for* MARTIN *to hear*). And our friend thinks the problem in this country is too much authority.

MARTIN. But still. I have decided. No.

MARTIN *makes to go.*

TRELAWNEY. Yes. I suppose it all depends on how serious you really are.

MARTIN. How serious I am?

TRELAWNEY. About the necessary consequences of what you want to bring about.

MARTIN. What necessary consequences?

JEREMY. Oh, Martin. What do you think will happen, when the free market is let rip? And the little firms go bankrupt, and unemployment rises and the welfare teat is pulled away and the plate glass is thrown up between 'the masses' and the goodies they've been promised as of right? Oh, and the steelworkers and the coal-miners and printers mobilise, to defend their privileges? I listen to the future and I'm hearing broken glass. I look into my crystal ball, and I see London burning. And if that happens, when that happens, what would you advise a British government to do? Surrender?

MARTIN. No, obviously not.

TRELAWNEY. No, you would advise it to defend the people it was elected to defend. The ordinary people who don't strike or riot. Who even now, are wondering how they will get to work tomorrow. Or, on the day after, what will happen to their savings and their homes. If not their country. Who have taken down the tree, and packed away the decorations, and wondered if there'll ever be another Christmas.

And if we elect a government that is not prepared to speak for them, to take on the enemy within, with the full force of the state and its authority, then, yes, I would call its commitment into question. It is after all, commitment that we are honouring, in Mr Lermontov.

Pause.

MARTIN. So who else is speaking at this ceremony?

TRELAWNEY. We are hoping that the actual presentation will be undertaken by Phyllis Weiner. Of Americans Against Surrender. Like you, a former radical. But on her own admission, moving rightwards steadily since 1952.

JEREMY. So, three defectors.

TRELAWNEY. Whose testimony is, thereby, uniquely credible. Having seen the future, and knowing where it leads.

JEREMY. And thus the urgency of stopping it.

MARTIN. And who's this message for? Who are you speaking to?

TRELAWNEY. Well, we hope, the next government of Britain.

Pause.

MARTIN. Look… look. I won't write your manifesto. And I'll say exactly what I think and feel.

TRELAWNEY. Of course.

MARTIN. But, as you say. For Lermontov.

TRELAWNEY. I am delighted.

A moment of relaxation. JEREMY *goes to refresh drinks.*

JEREMY. But, Martin, do you understand the full enormity of what is being asked of you?

TRELAWNEY, *a moment of alarm.*

MARTIN. What do you mean?

TRELAWNEY *gets it.*

TRELAWNEY. The ceremony is black tie.

CHORUS *and* PICKETS:

CHORUS. January 1979.

Hospitals refuse to treat all but emergencies.

Rat-infested rubbish piles up in Leicester Square.

Nearly thirty million days are lost to strikes.

PICKETS. What do we want? Revolution!

When do we want it? Now!

US out of Nicaragua!

US out of Salvador!

WEINER, *in her sixties, crosses the stage. She is aware the* PICKET *is directed at her.*

The People – United – will never be defeated.

El Pueblo – Unido – Nunca Sera Vencido!

Scene Four

A reception room adjacent to a banqueting hall in a large and expensive London hotel. A telephone on a small table. A large, dark, early-seventeenth-century painting on the wall. A WAITER *awaits, with sherries on a tray. There are two exits: one, left, into the banqueting hall, and the other, right, leading to the rest of the hotel.* WEINER *stands alone, smoking. She is in evening dress.*

WAITER. Sherry?

WEINER. What?

WAITER. Sherry, madam?

WEINER. Sure. Why not.

She takes a glass, as TRELAWNEY *enters, also in a dinner jacket, followed by* MARTIN.

TRELAWNEY. Look, I'm so sorry, we've completely lost the star attraction.

WEINER raises an eyebrow.

Present company excepted. Do you have a drink?

WEINER gestures with her glass. A noise in the corridor.

Aha.

He turns to the right entrance as PALOCZI *and*
LERMONTOV *come through it.* LERMONTOV *is in a*
strange, distant mood.

PALOCZI. Hugh, Pavel was at Bush House, it overran two
hours, I had to pick him up and change him in the cab –

WEINER (*to* LERMONTOV). Hallo, I'm Phyllis Weiner. It's a
privilege.

LERMONTOV *and* WEINER *shake hands.* TRELAWNEY
gestures to the WAITER, *who hands out sherry.*

LERMONTOV. I did an interview today, with the BBC Russian
Service. The interviewer was a man called Griboyedov. Very
strange. He seemed to think we fought on the wrong side in
the war.

Slight pause.

TRELAWNEY. Who's we?

LERMONTOV. You are.

Slight pause.

PALOCZI. He said nothing of the kind, Pavel. He wasn't
talking about Germany.

LERMONTOV. He was talking about siding with fascist states.

PALOCZI. He was talking about supporting the governments of
Chile and Brazil, against / insurgency –

LERMONTOV. And they're not fascists?

PALOCZI. Ask Professor Weiner. She has written quite
extensively on that very subject.

LERMONTOV *turns to* WEINER.

LERMONTOV. Well, then. Perhaps she will explain.

WEINER, *a quizzical look to* TRELAWNEY, *who makes no*
reaction.

WEINER. Well, in these times, I don't believe the West can
afford to be too, well, fastidious, about its choice of friends.

LERMONTOV. 'Objectively.'

WEINER. If we are not to end up living in a country like your country, Mr Lermontov.

The phone rings. TRELAWNEY *picks it up.*

TRELAWNEY. Hallo?

He puts his hand over the receiver.

Apparently, there's someone, in the lobby, who 'needs' to speak to Mr Lermontov.

PALOCZI *takes the phone.*

PALOCZI. Hallo, now what is this?

No, I'm not Lermontov, Mr Lermontov is about to go into dinner.

He slams the phone down.

People so slow and stupid in this country.

LERMONTOV *goes to the phone, picks it up and dials.*

LERMONTOV. Hallo, front desk? This is PM Lermontov. I would like the person who has come to see me sent up, please.

(*To* TRELAWNEY.) Where are we now?

TRELAWNEY. The Jacobean Suite. Um, I...

LERMONTOV (*down the phone*). The Jacobean Suite. Thank you.

He puts the phone down.

Please, start without me. I will miss the soup.

PALOCZI. Pavel –

LERMONTOV (*suddenly angry*). Do I have to spell it out in semaphore? Please, go away.

TRELAWNEY *and* WEINER *look at each other. An unspoken agreement.*

WEINER (*handing her glass back to the* WAITER). Thank you. Delicious.

> WEINER *and* TRELAWNEY *go out by the left door. Pause.* PALOCZI *takes out a pile of postcards, on which* LERMONTOV*'s speech is written.*

PALOCZI. We didn't have enough time in the taxi. You should look through these.

> MARTIN *goes.* PALOCZI *hands the cards to* LERMONTOV *and goes.* LERMONTOV *takes another drink from the* WAITER.

LERMONTOV. Thank you.

> *The* WAITER, *correctly, takes this as a dismissal, and goes out.* LERMONTOV *starts to look through the cards. A knock, right.*

LERMONTOV. Come in.

> *A woman* (CLARA) *in her mid-forties enters.*

Good evening, I am Lermontov.

CLARA. I know who you are.

LERMONTOV. Oh, you speak Russian?

CLARA. I'm sorry to disturb you. It was in the paper, you were here tonight.

LERMONTOV. I've only got a moment, I'm afraid...

CLARA. My name is Kaminskaya.

> *Pause.*

LERMONTOV. What?

CLARA. I work for TASS in London. Formerly I wrote things for *Isvestia*.

LERMONTOV. *Isvestia*?

CLARA. That's right.

LERMONTOV. You are CI Kaminskaya.

Pause.

CLARA. And formerly to that, attached to the Military
Intelligence Division of the Soviet Army. Stationed in
Budapest.

Pause.

Clara Ivanovna.

LERMONTOV. Oh, no.

CLARA. Do you remember?

LERMONTOV. You're in *London*?

CLARA. Yes.

LERMONTOV. This is – *preposterous*. The man is – *in there*.

CLARA. Who's in there?

LERMONTOV. The boy who I released, in Budapest. Who
threw the hand grenade.

CLARA. What hand grenade?

LERMONTOV *looks at* CLARA.

LERMONTOV. I am aware that there are grades. Levels of
invective. 'Childish, scurrilous and egotistical' for signing a
petition, 'hoarse, malicious and unsavoury' for an interview
with Western correspondents. But what you visited on me
broke all the rules. That wasn't from some well-thumbed
manual. That wasn't faceless. It was sharp and real, and
personal.

CLARA. Yes. It was personal.

LERMONTOV. Then, if it wasn't the boy with the grenade,
then – *why*?

CLARA. Because –

LERMONTOV. Why did you come here?

CLARA. Because you were coming here. Because you have been seduced into the camp of the most bellicose Cold War imperialists. And I did want to know –

LERMONTOV. 'The camp of the most bellicose – '

CLARA. Yes, the language is a little coarse. And arch. It's the vocabulary, in fact, of people who until quite recently were stupid peasants, working with wooden ploughs. Until they were all sent off to school.

LERMONTOV. Unless they starved to / death –

CLARA. One of the great achievements, you may think, of the Great October Revolution.

LERMONTOV. Please.

CLARA. I think often of my father. He served with a Komsomol detachment in the early thirties, laying pipelines across Russia's freezing wastes. He remembered it as among the best and most heroic times.

LERMONTOV. While, at the same time –

CLARA. You see, it isn't true, that the only way to get people to do anything is at the point of a bayonet. There are times when it isn't true.

LERMONTOV. This is absurd.

CLARA. What is absurd?

LERMONTOV. I am standing in a suite in a hotel in London, with a woman who put me in a labour camp.

CLARA. Well, now I have a face.

LERMONTOV. You knew *I* had a face.

CLARA. You're right. I'd seen it.

LERMONTOV. But you still –

CLARA. I'd seen it sneering in contempt, at a stupid girl from a Russian village, who knew nothing about music, who had never seen a city and who didn't always understand when people shouted at her very loud.

LERMONTOV. I see.

Pause.

Nine years.

Pause.

And you wanted me to see your face.

CLARA. No. I wanted to apologise.

Pause.

LERMONTOV. Why?

CLARA. Because it seems I have done something terrible.

LERMONTOV. What's that?

CLARA. I have driven a good Communist into the arms of those who think of others what I thought of you.

PALOCZI *enters.*

PALOCZI. Pavel, we cannot wait / any longer –

LERMONTOV. Well, there he is. The boy who I released. To whom I gave a hand grenade.

CLARA *looks at* PALOCZI, *then to* LERMONTOV, *and then goes out quickly.*

PALOCZI. Who was that woman?

LERMONTOV. Who is this man?

PALOCZI. What do you mean?

LERMONTOV. I mean, that since I came here, I have asked myself, what happened to the brave young revolutionary, who understood why peasants brought free food to feed the cities? Out of their hearts, not threatened by a bayonet?

PALOCZI. Pavel, you asked the crucial question.

LERMONTOV. Did I? What?

PALOCZI. 'How long d'you think they'll last?' The heroic peasants, in unshakable alliance with the equally unswerving working class? And I think you see the answer all around you.

Slight pause.

LERMONTOV. Yes, of course. 'The supine masses.' Let's go into dinner.

LERMONTOV *goes quickly out*. PALOCZI, *with a quizzical look, follows*.

Scene Five

The top table of the ceremony. Flowers bedeck, white linen gleams. JEREMY, TRELAWNEY, LERMONTOV, PALOCZI *and* MARTIN. *A statuette on a side table. A lectern.* TRELAWNEY *stands, and speaks into the microphone*.

TRELAWNEY. Professor Weiner.

*He sits.*WEINER *goes to the lectern*.

WEINER. Ladies and gentlemen. A story.

It's the story of my parents. Who, like so many others, fled Tsarist Russia – with its pogroms and its secret police – for the promised land of New York City. Worked hard, built up businesses. Lost everything, in the great depression. And looked to us – their children – to avenge their misery and suffering. Which we did by fighting for a better world. A world we thought was being built in the country which our folks had fled from. A new promised land.

While in fact it was already mounting trials and building camps and killing millions.

Which eventually, at last, too late, we admitted to the world and to ourselves. Thinking that if we bore witness to our terrible mistake, if we told it how it really was, our children would not follow us into the darkness.

But what happened was the opposite. A new generation, of apologists for tyranny. The campus radicals, the 'progressive intelligentsia'. Marching for American surrender in Vietnam. Marching for surrender now. And yes – many of them – were and are our children.

So it behooves us, once again, to tell it how it is.

Both MARTIN *and* LERMONTOV *are looking concerned at what* WEINER *is saying.*

To affirm that agitation's agitation, even if it's published quarterly in learned periodicals, and that subversion is subversion, even if the subverters of our culture are distinguished film directors, poets, writers and musicians. And that mobs of hooligans are mobs of hooligans, even if they happen to consist of college students and professors.

And that treachery is treachery, even if the traitors to our country have no need of tape machines and microfilm, but ply their trade as smart left lawyers, labour leaders, and conscience-striken academics.

PALOCZI *has been looking at a particular card in the pile. He removes it from the pile. He writes another card.*

And, worst of all, to admit that it's our fault. That we have spawned a generation so soft and effete, that they have lost the most important thing of all: I mean, a sense of who they really are.

I mean that it has taken me some time – it has taken me the best part of a lifetime – to admit, without embarrassment or hesitation: that I belong to the nation of my birth.

And if I may say so, Pavel Mikhailovich, it has taken you and people like you, voices issuing from the darkness of a nationhood suppressed, to convince me of that fact.

Applause, as PALOCZI *hands* LERMONTOV *the speech cards,* WEINER *picks up the statuette, and* LERMONTOV *stands to receive it.* WEINER *sits, and* LERMONTOV *goes to the lectern. He has to find somewhere to put the statuette down.*

LERMONTOV. Thank you. May I say first of all how good it is to spend an evening discussing freedom. Particularly as, in my country, no one is free to hold such a discussion. May I also thank the organisers for providing such a –

He turns and gestures with the card to PALOCZI.

What's this?

PALOCZI. Sumptuous?

LERMONTOV. Sumptuous – repast; and to Professor Weiner for such a generous and indeed inspiring speech. I think the phrase is: 'Follow that.'

And I must thank those gentlemen who selected me as a recipient of this award. I am most honoured. But I must say that I do not view this award as mine alone. I view it as being for all the zeks, in all the camps, the living and the dead.

New card:

For the violators, great and small, of the Criminal Code of the Russian Soviet Federative Socialist Republic.

He turns the card. Then realises this is where the removed card was in the pile. He goes quickly to PALOCZI, *takes the removed card from him, returns to the lectern and reads.*

From the agitators and subversives, violators of the public order, slanderers and hooligans and parasites and traitors, of the Soviet Corrective Labour Colonies.

Pause.

Who up until their sentences were writers, poets. Actors, film directors and musicians. Workers and trade-union officials. Students and professors.

A long pause, as LERMONTOV *looks through the rest of the cards. Then he places the cards on the table.*

It is not of course the same. It is not –

(*To* PALOCZI.) – equivalent, to be compared with?

Pause.

PALOCZI. Comparable.

LERMONTOV. Comparable. Of course. You have no camps. Your 'dissidents' are free. It is no way comparable.

And yet.

If you really want to see a nation, strong and tough and virile, marching to a single rhythm, banged out with a hammer on a rail, then – please – come to my country.

It is not that it's the same.

It's just – that it does appear to be – the same variety of people – who condemn it on the other side, but applaud it on their own.

And who – in less 'fastidious' times – might do to others what was done to me.

He picks up the statuette.

So. I am most honoured.

But I have decided. No. You will I hope forgive me.

LERMONTOV *returns the statuette to its place and goes quickly out.* TRELAWNEY *stands.*

TRELAWNEY. Ladies and gentlemen, the next –

But MARTIN *stands and goes out quickly, followed by* JEREMY. WEINER *lights a cigarette.*

Scene Six

Back in the Jacobean suite. MARTIN *enters, pursued by* JEREMY.

JEREMY. Martin, he's wrong. Just because he's suffered, just because he's brave, a hero, doesn't mean he can't be wrong.

MARTIN (*outburst*). I mean, come on, Jeremy, with hand on heart, do you really want a man like that to run the country?

JEREMY. Who?

MARTIN. We ditch the welfare, but we arm the state? We sack the nanny, hire a governess? Her job, to round up all the hooligans and agitators. Her motto, heed the mystic voices of our ancestors?

JEREMY. Martin. Sir Hugh is like he is because the enemy we face is like you were.

MARTIN. So, ultimately, actually, it's not about liberty at all. He said it, the market just the means. The end: authority and hierarchy and the country of our birth. And who can belong to it. And who's the human dust.

Pause. JEREMY *changes tone.*

JEREMY. It's odd, you come to realise, it's really not the flags and fanfares. It's the little things. The sensual things. The smell of woodsmoke. Mulled wine, warming chilly fingers. The family's wellingtons, all lined up in the hall. But that come the crunch, yes, you would take up arms, you'll maim and kill, to keep those things. The part of you you value most. The part that you rejected, but I never had, you see.

MARTIN. What are you saying?

JEREMY. Take the last step, Martin. No more pretence. Be who you are.

Go home.

Pause. Enter TRELAWNEY.

TRELAWNEY. Well?

The CHORUS*:*

CHORUS. May 1979: Margaret Thatcher wins the General Election.

June 1980: It's announced that American cruise missiles are to be deployed at RAF Greenham Common, Berkshire.

Summer 1981: There are riots across Britain, including Brixton, Liverpool and Birmingham.

March 1982: The first blockade of the Greenham Common base takes place, and there are thirty-four arrests.

November 1983: The first cruise missiles are deployed.

A YOUNG WOMAN *with pink hair is manhandled off the stage by a* POLICEMAN.

Scene Seven

Summer. 1984. MARTIN*'s mother's home.* MARTIN *stands, with a whisky and a cigarette, looking at a photograph.* AMANDA *stands in woolly socks. Her muddy wellingtons are nearby.*

MARTIN. That's her?

AMANDA. Yup.

MARTIN (*with a 'phew'*). And have they charged her?

AMANDA. Yes. With threatening behaviour.

MARTIN. On my land?

AMANDA. Not on 'your land'.

MARTIN. So let me get this straight –

AMANDA. The land was common. The land between your house and the perimeter of the US Air Force base. Last

week, the council repossessed the land – surely, they told
you? – and sold it to the base. So yesterday, at dawn, the
women were ejected, Tanya was arrested, and that fence was
built. So hence, today –

MARTIN. I have fairies at the bottom of my garden.

AMANDA *breathes deeply*.

Apparently, to get rid of them, I have to file a formal
complaint.

AMANDA. And will you?

MARTIN (*looking at the photo*). You know, there's this little,
stained-glass St Anne, in the Lady Chapel of our church, the
spit... that is, without the pink hair.

AMANDA. You go to church?

MARTIN. I'm the anchor of the baritones. We only get a
service every other week, but the padre is a sound, no-
nonsense chap. Soup only to the conspicuously needy.
Lucky, because in Lower Purley they've this bloke who
appears to think Pol Pot was basically sound, just a little soft
on the urban middle class. So what's your present bag, then?
Apart, that is, from Battered Lesbians Against the Bomb?

Pause.

AMANDA. I'm running a resources centre.

She hands him a leaflet.

MARTIN. Well well well. I run a XJ12. Look, I'm sorry, do you
want a drink?

AMANDA. No thanks.

MARTIN. A fag?

AMANDA. You haven't given up?

MARTIN. Not that, at least.

(*Re: the leaflet.*) So what in God's name is 'alternative
technology'? From whom does who wish to 'reclaim the
night'?

AMANDA (*heading off to her boots*). I'm sorry, I can't do this.

MARTIN *goes and pours* AMANDA *a drink.*

MARTIN. Please.

AMANDA (*putting on her boots*). They're clearing space around the hangers. Apparently, that usually means there's an alert.

MARTIN (*glance at his watch*). That always means there's an alert.

He holds the drink out to her.

Five minutes.

A moment. AMANDA *glances at her muddy boots.* MARTIN *smiles and shrugs.* AMANDA *comes and gets the drink.*

AMANDA. Why the fuck not.

MARTIN. And presumably you were unflinchingly opposed to our rescuing our kith and kin on the Falkland Islands?

AMANDA. I didn't quite see why we had to mount a war.

MARTIN. And equally implacable in your support for the striking miners?

AMANDA. And their families. And their communities.

MARTIN. And their right to keep bankrupt coal mines open for eternity.

AMANDA. And you're all right with what the police are doing to prevent them? 'By any / means necessary'?

MARTIN. – means necessary –

AMANDA. And so all the Falklands flagwaving, and the pigs fanning out across the country like / an army –

MARTIN. – an invading army –

AMANDA. – and the reassertion of our / imperial –

MARTIN. National pride.

AMANDA. I was going to say 'imperial spirit', all to make the nation safe for private enterprise?

MARTIN. Well, no, not / just...

AMANDA. No, because, actually, to make it safe for the police. For tradition, discipline and order. Freed of permissiveness and women being uppity and being swamped by alien cultures and the enemy within. Not how it could be. How it was.

MARTIN. And don't you think, that's how people want it?

He goes to replenish his drink.

AMANDA. Martin. I once told you how I used to cry.

MARTIN. Did you?

AMANDA. Me and my child, our noses pressed against the lighted windows, watching the two-point-four kids playing round the Christmas tree.

MARTIN *turns back to her.*

Thinking, why me? Why couldn't *I* accept things as they were? Why did *I* have to feel it was all wrong, and that I was put into the world to set it right?

Well, you know as well as I do. All those opportunities, those bold bright hospitals and schools and universities. That our folks had never had themselves, but had been through a slump and then a war to win for us. And if we don't protect that, if we don't complete the building of the New Jerusalem, for them, for us, then yes, maybe they'll turn back to faith and flag and send 'em home, and we'll deserve it.

MARTIN. And of course I never felt like that. Being 'what I am'.

AMANDA. Well, did you?

Pause.

So. Are you going to call the police?

MARTIN. How long?

AMANDA. How long?

MARTIN. Do you think you'll last? A week? A month? For ever?

Suddenly, a LOUDSPEAKER *blares.* AMANDA *hurries out into the garden.* MARTIN *stands with his Scotch, looking at the picture of* TANYA*'s arrest.*

LOUDSPEAKER. Scorcher. We have Scorcher. I repeat, we have a Scorcher.

Sirens begin to wail. Dogs bark. Engines rev. Searchlights flare. Headlamps, of trucks and motorcycles.

Cresta Run. We are go for Cresta Run.

The lights dazzle the audience. Engines revving wildly.

Kiss. We are Kiss. Repeat, all units. We are Kiss.

The sirens fade. The headlamps and searchlights die, as the 'vehicles' reverse away. MARTIN *lights a cigarette. Perhaps we hear 'I Vow to Thee, My Country'.*

Scene Eight

MARTIN. Martin will remain a Conservative pundit, and will become active in the Countryside Alliance. He will fail to give up smoking.

AMANDA. He will die on 10th September, 2001.

JEREMY. Jeremy will write a major study of the works of AE Housman, during which his opinion of the poet will decline. His opinions on all other matters will remain the same.

AMANDA. In 1985, Amanda will start training as a psychotherapist.

JUDY. Judy will serve on the Greater London Council until its abolition in 1986.

TRELAWNEY. Lord Trelawney of Tintagel will produce a book entitled *Albion Redux*. He will die on the same day as Princess Diana.

BRYONY. Bryony will train as a solicitor and will be part of the legal team supporting the Stephen Lawrence's family during the Macpherson Inquiry into his murder.

LERMONTOV. Pavel Lermontov will support the anti-Communist revolutions in Eastern Europe and Russia, but will express concern about the speed and corruption of the subsequent market reforms. He will complete new Russian translations of the novels of Jane Austen.

CLARA. Clara Kaminskaya will oppose the Gorbachev reforms and the break-up of her country. She will set up a small museum devoted to the Soviet Space Programme.

JAMES. James Grain will participate in the planning of the 2003 demonstration against the invasion of Iraq. He will leave Socialist Vanguard when it fails to confront sexual harassment by and of its members.

KOROLENKO. Oleksander Korolenko will return to Ukraine. He will participate in both the Orange Revolution of 2004 and the Maidan uprising of 2014.

PALOCZI. Miklos Paloczi will return to Hungary and become an advisor to its government, on issues relating to immigration and nationality.

WEINER. Phyllis Weiner will strive to persuade her party not to select Donald Trump, but will vote for him in the 2016 Presidential Election.

PHIL. Phil will set up a housing campaign group called Roof Right, and will receive an MBE. He will return it in protest against the Grenfell fire.

AMANDA. Martin will give up smoking.

MARTIN. He will support the invasion of Iraq, but will be troubled by the lack of planning for its post-war future. In 2015, he will visit the Calais jungle. In 2017, he will abstain in what he will see as an unnecessary General Election. He will spend a week in Hungary.

AMANDA. Amanda will write an influential report on self-harm amongst teenage girls. She and Martin will not have spoken since 1984.

MARTIN. But she and Tanya will sometimes receive a Christmas card.

TANYA *is the young woman with pink hair.*

TANYA. Tanya will become a priest in the Church of England. She will vote remain in 2016 and Liberal Democrat in 2017. Her daughter Anne will become an LGBTQIA activist, live in France, and participate in protests at the University of Nanterre. Next year, she will join a Europe-wide campaign called A Future without Frontiers.

AMANDA. She will recruit her grandmother.

TANYA. She will campaign in Warsaw, Malmo and Budapest, where she'll be arrested.

AMANDA. She will be attacked by anti-immigration demonstrators in Lubeck, East Germany.

TANYA. And she will write to Martin.

MARTIN *opens a letter.*

CHORUS. Mayday.

Mayday.

Mayday.

MARTIN *looks at the letter.*

The word 'Mayday' echoes around the theatre.

End of play.

Timeline 1945–1984

1945

May	Nazi Germany surrenders to the victorious British, American, French and Soviet armies.
July	The British Labour Party wins a landslide general election victory.
August	Atom bombs dropped on two Japanese cities bring the Second World War to an end.

1947

August	India wins independence from Britain.

1948

February	A Communist regime takes over Czechoslovakia.
June	The Soviet Union blockades West Berlin and an airlift is mounted to supply the city.
July	The British National Health Service is founded.

1949

October	The Chinese Communist Revolution is proclaimed.

1950

June	The Korean War breaks out, between the Communist-backed North and the Western-backed South of the divided country.

1954

May   In Vietnam, the Communist Viet Minh guerrillas
             defeat the French at the battle of Dien Bien Phu.

1955

December   Civil rights activist Rosa Parks refuses to give up
             her seat to a white passenger on a bus in Alabama.

1956

February   Nikita Kruschchev condemns Stalin at the
             Twentieth Congress of the Soviet Communist
             Party.

October   British and French troops invade Suez.

November   Soviet troops invade Hungary.

1958

February   The British Campaign for Nuclear Disarmament
             (CND) is founded.

1959

February   Fidel Castro takes power in Cuba.

1960

March   Sixty-nine black South Africans are killed in the
             Sharpeville Massacre.

November   John F. Kennedy is elected American President.

1961

August   The Berlin Wall is constructed, dividing east
             Berlin from west.

September   Mass arrests are made during an anti-nuclear
             sit-down in Trafalgar Square.

1962

February   Six CND activists are jailed for occupying the Air
             Force base at Wethersfield.

October   The Cuban Missile Crisis brings the world to the
             brink of nuclear catastrophe.

1963

August   Martin Luther King delivers his 'I have a dream'
             speech in Washington.

November   President Kennedy is assassinated.

1964

August   Three civil rights workers are murdered in
             Mississippi.

October   Nikita Krushchev falls from power and Leonid
             Brezhnev succeeds him as General Secretary of
             the Soviet Communist Party.

1965

March   Civil rights marchers are attacked by police on a
             bridge in Selma, Alabama.

November   The Pentagon is immobilised by anti-Vietnam War
             protestors.

1966

February	Soviet dissident writers Andrei Sinyavksy and Yuli Daniel are sentenced to labour camps for publishing their writings in the west.
October	The Black Panther Party is founded in Oakland, California.

1967

January	Dissidents demonstrate in Moscow's Pushkin Square against the tightening of the Soviet criminal code.
April	Right-wing colonels take over the Greek government in a military coup.
July	Black protestors riot in Detroit and Newark.
October	Cuban revolutionary Che Guevara is killed in Bolivia.

1968

January	The Viet Cong invades Saigon in the Tet (New Year) Offensive.
March	Violence breaks out during a demonstration outside the American Embassy in London's Grovesnor Square.
	Lyndon Johnson withdraws from the 1968 Presidential race.
April	Martin Luther King is assassinated and riots break out across America.
	Enoch Powell delivers his 'rivers of blood' speech against commonwealth immigration to Britain.
May	A student uprising in Paris provokes a general strike in France.

June   Senator Robert Kennedy is assassinated.

August   Soviet troops invade Czechoslovakia. Soviet
                dissidents protest in Red Square: they are arrested
                and exiled or imprisoned.

                Riots break out at the Democratic Party
                convention in Chicago.

November   President Richard Nixon is elected.

1969

August   500,000 attend the rock festival at Woodstock in
                upstate New York.

                British troops are sent into Northern Ireland.

September   Inspired by student protests, Italy's 'hot autumn'
                of strikes begins.

1970

March   Three anti-war revolutionaries are blown up by
                their own bomb in New York City.

April   American troops invade Cambodia.

May   During protest demonstrations, six students are
                killed at Kent State and Jackson State
                universities.

June   A mass campaign leads to the cancellation of a
                British tour by an all-white South African cricket
                team.

                In a surprise victory by the British Conservatives,
                Edward Heath is elected Prime Minister, and
                pledges to limit the power of the trade unions.

September   Marxist Salvador Allende is elected President of
                Chile.

November   The Miss World contest at the Albert Hall is disrupted by women protestors and a BBC outside broadcast van is attacked.

December   Strikes in Poland lead to the resignation of the Communist Party leader.

1971

January   The Angry Brigade urban guerrilla group bombs the home of the British Employment Minister in protest against the Government's Industrial Relations Act.

June   The Upper Clyde shipbuilders' work-in begins in Scotland.

The underground magazine *Oz* is put on trial for obscenity.

August   Internment without trial is introduced in Northern Ireland.

1972

January   A national miners' strike leads to blackouts across Britain.

On Bloody Sunday, fourteen Catholic civilians are killed by British paratroops in Derry.

The Strategic Arms Limitation Agreement signals the beginning of détente between the United States and the Soviet Union.

February   The miners win their seven-week strike.

March   Direct rule from Westminster is imposed on Northern Ireland.

June   Employees of the Nixon White House break into the Watergate headquarters of the Democratic Party.

Five dockers are jailed in Pentonville for defying the Industrial Relations Act; they are released after strikes and mass protests.

December In the Angry Brigade trial, four people are convicted and jailed, four are aquitted.

1973

March The IRA bombs the Old Bailey in London.

April Nixon White House aides resign over the thickening Watergate scandal.

May Two million workers strike on May Day.

September President Allende is overthrown and killed during a military coup in Chile.

October Israel wins the Yom Kippur War against the surrounding Arab states; an embargo leads to the quadrupling of the price of oil.

December The miners impose a work-to-rule, and a three-day working week is introduced.

1974

February Prime Minister Edward Heath calls a General Election on the slogan: 'Who governs Britain?'; the Conservatives lose to Labour, and the miners win their strike.

Dissident writer Alexander Solzhenitsyn is expelled from the Soviet Union.

April Fascism is overthrown in Portugal.

July Military rule ends in Greece.

August President Nixon resigns over the Watergate cover-up.

1975

February	Margaret Thatcher defeats Edward Heath to become Conservative Party Leader.
April	Communist forces take over South Vietnam and Cambodia.
June	Britain votes 'yes' in a referendum on its membership of the European Economic Community.
November	Spanish dictator General Franco dies.

1976

June	Following an uprising led by schoolchildren, at least a hundred and seventy-six protestors are killed by the South African police in Soweto.
August	Riots break out at London's Notting Hill Carnival.
September	Chinese leader Chairman Mao Zedong dies, and his 'Gang of Four' supporters are arrested.
December	Soviet dissident Vladimir Bukovsky is released from prison camp and deported to the West, in exchange for Chilean Communist leader Luis Corvalán.

1977

January	Czech dissidents publish the human-rights manifesto Charter 77.
June	Mass pickets support a strike for unionisation of the Grunwick Film Processing Plant in North London.
September	Anti-Apartheid activist Steve Biko dies in detention in South Africa.

1978

March	Aldo Moro, former Italian Prime Minister, is kidnapped and killed by the Red Brigades.
April	100,000 anti-fascists attend an Anti-Nazi-League Carnival in East London.
July	Soviet dissidents Alexander Ginzburg and Natan Sharansky are sentenced to long terms in labour camps.
December	Vietnamese troops invade Cambodia and overthrow the Khmer Rouge regime.

1979

January	Public sector workers mount a wave of strikes against a government pay-cap, dubbed the Winter of Discontent.
February	The Shah of Iran is deposed.
April	Activist Blair Peach dies from injuries received during an anti-National Front demonstration in Southall, London.
May	Margaret Thatcher is elected Prime Minister.
November	The American Embassy in Teheran is seized by Iranian demonstrators and its staff taken hostage.
December	The USSR commits troops to support the Communist government of Afghanistan.

1980

August	Strikes in the Gdansk shipyard lead to the founding of the independent trade union Solidarity in Poland.
November	Ronald Reagan is elected President of the United States.

1981

February	The Social Democratic Party is founded in Britain.
May	In Belfast, IRA prisoners go on hunger strike in their campaign for political status.
	A left-wing group led by Ken Livingstone takes over the Greater London Council.
July	Riots in London, Liverpool and Manchester.
September	The Labour Party votes for unilateral nuclear disarmament.

1982

February	Women blockade Greenham Common Air Force base in protest against the decision to deploy American cruise missiles.
May	Following the Argentinian invasion of the Falkland Islands, a British naval task force is despached to win them back.
June	Israeli forces invade southern Lebanon.
October	The Polish government outlaws the Solidarity trade union.
November	Leonid Brezhnev dies and Yuri Andropov takes over as leader of the USSR.

1983

March	President Reagan denounces the Soviet bloc as an 'evil empire'.
June	Margaret Thatcher is re-elected in a landslide.
July	The United States increases its support for the rebels against the left-wing Sandinista government in Nicaragua.

December   Polish Solidarity leader Lech Wałęsa receives the
Nobel Peace Prize in absentia.

Following the arrival of American cruise missiles,
fifty thousand women protestors encircle the
Greenham Common base.

1984

March   Britain's miners go on strike against pit closures.

TRYING IT ON

To Dan Rebellato

Characters

DAVID
OLDER
YOUNGER

All three parts are played by the same person.

Setting

A study, full of cardboard boxes, ring files, box files, filing
cabinets, on to which it is possible to project images.
A microphone. The stage manager's table to the side.

Note on Text

Lines in italics are recorded speech.

Scene One: Warnings

DAVID. If this was a play, it would be clearer when it had started.

The lights would go down.

I wouldn't have to introduce Danni our stage manager.

Because there'd be a programme.

And if it was a play by me, there'd probably be warnings. Which is often a issue between playwrights and management.

And although I've had smoke and flashing lights and nudity in my plays, involving people of both sexes, you'll be relieved to hear not this one, my big problem's been with armaments. So when the RSC did my play *Pentecost* – which is about a fresco in an East European church, which is taken over by asylum seekers – there was a big debate about whether we should warn about gunfire.

And there were two things. One is that if you draw attention to upcoming gunfire, as soon as anything vaguely cylindrical appears on the stage, people start wincing and sucking their teeth. But the other thing is that, in *Pentecost*, if you know there's gunfire then there comes a point when you know how the play is going to end.

So we negotiated. And we thought about kind of obscuring what was going to happen, either by generalisation ('*Pentecost* includes effects'),

equivocation ('*Pentecost* may contain gunfire'),

or camouflage ('*Pentecost* contains some but not all of the following…').

But then something struck me. Maybe we're looking at this thing the wrong way round. Far from warning too much, might we be warning too little?

Aren't there things people have a right to know about, beyond smoke and bangs?

'This production has at least one catastrophic piece of miscasting.'

'There is a significant longeur towards the beginning of Act Two.'

'The management *knows* about the lighting.'

So. You may be invited to answer challenging and potentially revealing questions.

The actor has not acted since he played Captain Bligh in a university production of *The Mutiny on the Bounty*.

He hasn't even learnt his lines, and is thus reliant on potentially hostile technology. But in very capable hands.

Slight pause.

There will be elements of self-exposure.

Things remembered may be things imagined.

If this was a play, or a certain sort of play, its written text would start with a stage direction.

Scene Two: Room

A projection: the Birmingham skyline.

DAVID. An old man in a room at the top of his house. The window looks out over what might seem a contradiction in terms: a breathtaking view of the Birmingham skyline.

In front of the window is a desk, with a pair of filing cabinets at right angles to one side, and a green-baize-topped card table on the other, forming a kind of console, which surrounds him as he sits on his orthopaedic chair.

He wheels the chair to the centre.

On the desk, there is the remnant of a cigarette burn which dates the desk from at least before the 28th of March 1984.

But the most striking thing about the room is that it's full of paper, mostly but not all in ring files, box files, and cardboard boxes, in which are large manilla envelopes, stuffed with cuttings. And for papers which haven't quite yet found a home, or are between homes, piles.

The man is seventy. And the cardboard box he visits most now – both to add to it and to consult it – was marked Euro Pop-Right and was then marked Euro Pop-Right Brexit and now Euro Pop-Right Brexit Trump. And while these phenomena are generally worrying they are particularly so for someone who was twenty in 1968, fifty years ago, the *annus mirabilis* of the international student revolutionary left.

On the day that Hitler came to power, Goebbels said: 'the year 1789' – the year of the French Revolution – 'is hereby eradicated from history.' You could say that the political project of Euro Pop-Right Brexit Trump is to do the same to 1968.

And there's a particular irony in this. The year he was elected, Donald Trump was seventy.

Scene Three: First Survey

DAVID *opens a filing cabinet and takes out a clipboard.*

DAVID. Can I ask you some questions?

House lights up.

How many people in this room vote the same way as at least one of their parents? Show of hands.

Danni, could we have it a bit brighter?

House lights up further.

How many people have voted for more than one party?

How many people have ever voted Conservative?

How many people voted Brexit?

Well, that's it. A completely representative sample. That's if you are all telling the truth, which of course you are.

Now. Here's a list of six characteristics of voters in the 2016 EU referendum.

What I want to know is which of these characteristics would make someone *least* likely to vote Brexit, and which one *most*.

He reads out a list, which is projected on the set.

One: Having a household income under twenty thousand pounds.
Two: Having voted Labour in 2015.
Three: Being sixty-five or over.
Four: Having a degree.
Five: Being in paid work.
Six: Thinking capitallism is a force for ill.

That's capitalism with one L.

So what was the factor that made people least likely to vote Leave?

He takes suggestions from the audience.

Voting Labour in 2015.

Lest we forget, Labour delivered two-thirds of its vote to Remain, whereas nearly sixty per cent of Tory voters defied the advice of their party leader.

And what did people think was the most likely factor to make people vote Leave?

He takes suggestions from the audience.

Being sixty-five or over.

Leavers were not by and large working-class Labour voters from the north of England.

What they were was old. And old people are less likely than young people to be have a degree. They're poorer. And more likely to support bringing back blue passport covers and the death penalty.

Nearly sixty per cent of sixty-five-plussers were between fifteen and twenty-five in 1968.

He puts the clipboard back in the filing cabinet and kicks it shut.

So, what happened to the Sergeant Pepper generation?

Why, fifty years on, does it seem to him that the political gains of that generation are going to be reversed, and the people who're reversing them are the people that he thought those gains were for?

Scene Four: Backgrounds

DAVID. And so he sets to, to discover. He does what he always does. He reads books, watches documentaries, goes through files of newspaper cuttings and conducts interviews, largely with people who, like him, came of age between 'Love Me Do' and 'Let It Be'.

He asks about the kinds of backgrounds the people came from, and how that had influenced their politics. This is Martin Jacques, who went on to edit the journal *Marxism Today*.

Projections of the interviewees appear on the set.

MARTIN JACQUES. *Well, both my parents worked during the war at Armstrong Siddeley, which was an aircraft factory in Coventry. And they joined the Communist Party in that period.*

DAVID. And this is David Aaronovitch, of *The Times*, also from a Communist family:

DAVID AARONOVITCH. *Some of the people we had coming into the house were delightful people. But it was always really the Russians. I was on the side of the Russians. I knew every kind of aeroplane flown in the second world war.*

DAVID. Paul Mason the economist, he's a bit younger.

PAUL MASON. *Well, my family background is unusual because half of them are miners and weavers from Lancashire and half of them are Jewish tailors who went from somewhere in Russia via New York City and came to Liverpool.*

DAVID. Sue Clegg, who's a lecturer in Leeds.

SUE CLEGG. *All my dad's side was all miners… So there's no doubt about working-class consciousness, is what I'm saying. And I knew I had to get out, cos I knew in those communities what happened to girls was, you got trapped.*

DAVID. And Brian Goodwin and Jill Ambler, two friends from Birmingham.

BRIAN GOODWIN. *My father – and obviously my mother – were involved in the general strike.*

JILL AMBLER. *My father was the fourth son of a Baptist Minister, of a Strict and Particular Baptist Minister.*

DAVID. And Hilary Wainwright's father was a Liberal MP.

HILARY WAINWRIGHT. *But I could see there that the radicalism of my father – because he was quite a radical Liberal – was not consistent with capitalism and therefore it was like a dead-end to remain in the Liberal Party.*

DAVID. 1968 revolutionary leader Tariq Ali, who was brought up in Pakistan:

TARIQ ALI. *I grew up in a strange atmosphere, which was largely meeting Communist intellectuals, trade unionists, peasant leaders, and occasionally meeting people from a completely different background who were in some shape or form running the country.*

DAVID. And I asked them whether their politics arose out of their personal experience.

PAUL MASON. *So I went to a Catholic grammar school, and almost, you know, if you want to decipher the subtext of a what a Catholic grammar school, it's just two lessons: don't have sex and don't become a Marxist.*

DAVID. And whether there was a 'road to Damascus' moment, when they thought: 'Hey, I've become a revolutionary.'

DAVID AARONOVITCH. *I never didn't think that I would… This was what you did politically, this was where I stood, emotionally and politically.*

DAVID. Not any more

DAVID AARONOVITCH. *There comes a point when you have to say to yourself, 'No, I don't actually think that the Russian system is superior.'*

DAVID. While, for Brian…

BRIAN GOODWIN. *So I cajoled and bullied… So we went on strike, for half a day, for an afternoon, we all walked out. It was brilliant.*

DAVID. Another factory in Coventry. And he became a member of the International Socialists. Like Sue Clegg.

SUE CLEGG. *I did actually feel I was becoming a revolutionary.*

DAVID. And there were many feminists. Sarah Braun, in Bristol.

SARAH BRAUN. *My mother's mother was a suffragette. So I was ready for the women's movement.*

DAVID. And Anna Coote, who was a student journalist and then went on to the *Observer*.

ANNA COOTE. *I would have been about maybe twenty. And we had to go and look for things in the library which was in another part of the building.*

DAVID. And to get there she had to walk through the compositors' room, which was full of big burly blokes operating the machines.

ANNA COOTE. *And what they did, when I appeared at one end of the room, was to set up a whistle. And then they would all take it up, until when you got to the other end of the room, everyone was whistling at me. I found this profoundly embarrassing. Absolutely paralysing embarrassing.*

DAVID. And he spoke to people – politics students, at Warwick University, who are twenty today. And one of them said something that could have been said any time in the last fifty years:

'To use an age-old phrase of the left', he said, 'I would just like to look back and feel like I was on the right side of history. Not being correct per se. I was out there for good reason. I was fighting for a good cause.'

He turns to the projections. The photographs of the interviewees now mix into photographs of them in their twenties. He turns back.

But it strikes him that there's one person he hasn't interviewed, because he can't.

Scene Five: Self-Portraiture

DAVID. When you look at classical self-portraits, you're warned against reading these paintings as a psychological study by the painter of himself. In fact, in the seventeenth century, the purpose of self-portraiture was essentially technical; it was to try out poses, gestures, expressions, costumes on a model you didn't have to pay. To see this as an autobiographical project, so the argument runs, is to impose a contemporary consciousness on the past.

Well, I have my doubts about this theory.

Twenty years ago, I am in a room in the Louvre, in front of two Rembrandt self-portraits, both of which were painted in 1633, when he was twenty-seven.

The two portraits are projected.

In the first of these pictures Rembrandt is wearing a hat with
a thin gold chain around the brim, with a more elaborate gold
chain slung jauntily around his neck. His expression is alert,
faintly superior; his moustache perky. The second portrait is
hatless, the brow furrowed, in a more defensive pose; the
shoulder is turned agains the viewer, the chain is hung
straighter, less flamboyantly, perhaps more securely. It's
anxious, but openly so. Going back to the first one, I notice
something else. In shadow, just at the bottom, a hand is
gripping the chain. And in fact, the eyes don't look directly
at you. Then back to the second portrait. Its gaze is even
more direct, no-nonsense, unambiguous. Now the first
portrait looks *really* shifty. As if the second portrait has seen
through the first. What is he clutching? Is it *his* gold chain?
Who's he trying to kid? What is he trying on?

The Rembrandts disappear. Now we see a mute clip of
DAVID, *aged thirty-one, talking on 'Nickleby & Co.', a*
South Bank Show *special.*

The old man in the attic room sometimes thinks that a young
man might be downstairs, wondering what his portrait would
look like now.

He turns and sees the image of himself.

This the earliest bit of videotape available of him in
adulthood. It's from an interview about his 1980 RSC
adaptation of *Nicholas Nickleby*, which is going to be his
biggest commercial success. Which of course he doesn't
know yet.

*During this, he goes and looks at the clip on the stage
manager's laptop.*

DAVID (*on* The South Bank Show). *So that's a daunting
prospect. But what I've got to be very careful of is not to go
into every scene and ask, 'How can I make this shorter?',
not for that to be the kind of dominating thing, looking at any
chapter, saying, 'How can I make this a quarter of the
length?'*

DAVID *watches himself. The sound fades, as he speaks.*

Because that would end up with, would actually end up with something which is very, that would lose the magic of the book. The great problem with Dickens is that all one's instincts…

DAVID. He pushes his glasses up his nose a lot. He pushes my glasses up his nose a lot. I push my glasses up my nose a lot.

He's the YOUNGER DAVID.

Scene Six: Damascus

DAVID *takes a frock coat from a clothes hook.*

DAVID. And so, in 1966, I am eighteen. And much to my father's irritation, I grow my hair and buy a Victorian frock coat, three wing collars, two cravats, and a cravat pin.

He puts on the coat.

It is in this Wildean persona that I intend to take the University of Manchester by storm.

I come to the attention of the student newspaper. I raise eyebrows at my hall of residence, and I'm asked by a fellow drama student if I'm for real. It's a good question.

He takes off the coat.

Eighteen months later, I'm editor of the student newspaper, and campaigning for the reinstatement of two students who have been expelled for shouting down the Secretary of State for Education. Although the two students are members of the revolutionary International Socialists, later to become the Socialist Workers' Party – not to be confused with the International Marxist Group or the Socialist Labour League or the University Socialist Society – I don't support them for that reason. I see this as an issue of the right to protest.

And then I hit Damascus.

It must be the first week of April, 1968. I think it's in the Student Union cafeteria, with its long formica-topped tables. A student I know is sitting there.

MARTIN JACQUES. *Dave Clark? Do you remember Dave Clark? Interesting guy. Breath of fresh air. Didn't have that sort of tribalism of the left.*

A clip from World in Action. DAVE CLARK *heads a demonstration in Manchester. Elsewhere on the set, we see footage from the Grovesnor Square demonstration of 17th March 1968.*

DAVE CLARK *(speaking on a bus going to the demonstration). So I think the time has come for all of us – or for the many of us who feel like me – to unite and bring about a radical social change, then if violence is a part of it, violence is a part of it.*

DAVID. He was on the 17th March 1968 Vietnam demo, the one that ended with pitched battles between demonstrators and the police, in Grovesnor Square. He was, I wasn't.

He calls me over to his table, to congratulate me on a speech I made in the Students' Union in support of the two expelled students. But he has something else to say.

Isn't it time that I got serious and joined the revolution?

And I think I stutter about violence and the dictatorship of the proletariat and means not justifying ends. I say I'm for peace in Vietnam, not necessarily for the other side, not for the Communists to win.

And I imagine but I don't remember him putting a picture on the table.

He takes a number of identical cards from a filing cabinet. The cards show Eddie Adams' picture of the shooting of a Viet Cong guerrilla in the streets of Saigon, on 1st February, 1968. Behind him, the photograph is projected on the set.

He asks me: 'What are you looking at?'

During this, he throws down copies of the photograph. At the same time, the projected photograph zooms in, becoming larger and larger.

I'll tell you what you think you're looking at. A man shot dead at point-blank range, in the streets of Saigon.

Now let me tell you three things. First, the guy doing the shooting is a general, the Chief of the South Vietnamese police. So it's a man shot dead by a cop at point-blank range.

The second thing is the man isn't posing any kind of threat. His hands are tied. It's a public street.

It's a man shot dead by a cop in cold blood at point-blank range.

He's unarmed.

So, he's an innocent man shot dead by a cop in cold blood at point-blank range.

How could anyone commit such a ghastly act of criminal brutality?

Except that isn't what's happening. The guy being shot is an officer in the National Liberation Front. The Viet Cong. The Communists. His squad has been killing people all day. Earlier, they broke into the compound of the US Embassy.

So the question that this picture asks you isn't, how could somebody behave so brutally and heartlessly and blah blah blah. It's how could a peasant army of little yellow people in black pyjamas invade the headquarters of the most powerful military machine on earth.

The answer? They have the overwhelming support of the Vietnamese masses.

That's what you're looking at. The unstoppable force of the heroic Vietnamese.

He throws down the last copy. The last zoom in on the projection.

'Come on, Uncle, let's get serious.'

He calls me 'Uncle'.

Scene Seven: Heroes

DAVID. And it's just a few days later when Martin Luther King is assassinated and cities across America erupt in flames. In May, the Paris student uprising which provokes a general strike. In October, two American sprinters on the Mexico Olympic medal podium raise their black-gloved fists in protest against racism.

A projection of Tommy Smith and John Carlos, holding up their fists on the Mexico City podium, in October 1968. DAVID picks up a black glove and looks at it. Then.

And Dave moves in. And we print the *Socialist Society* – or *Soc Soc* – magazine on an ancient Roneo duplicator in our bathroom.

And then, in February 1969, *Soc Soc* is mounting a campaign for the reform – well, abolition – of the examination system. And there's a ballot for a student boycott of all classes if our demands aren't met. In the last three days of the campaign for yes, we produce a daily leaflet.

He takes copies of the leaflets from cardboard boxes and piles them round the set.

The last one, on the actual ballot day, will go to every student in the university, under doors of rooms in every hall of residence, handed out outside every lecture theatre or department building or laboratory.

The 'shhhh shhhh' of the duplicator.

There's ten thousand students, and the leaflet's two sides with two colours on each side.

He pulls out a clothing line with used stencils hanging on it.

Splattered like bloody bandages with red correcting fluid –
which can give you a slight high – stencils hang on washing
lines as we change the colour drum. An hour into the
duplicating process the electrical element in our third-hand
Roneo gives up.

The 'shhh shhh' stops.

We're faced with nearly forty thousand manual turns of the
duplicator's handle.

The 'shhh shhh' starts again.

The blokes do it in twenty-minute shifts while the girls make
coffee and pass cooling hands across our brows.

At 6 a.m., when the distributors arrive to collect the leaflets,
we're finished.

He looks at the glove.

It is among the happiest nights of my life.

He puts on the glove.

I've tried it on. It fits.

Scene Eight: Armour

DAVID *tentatively raises his black-gloved fist in salute.*

DAVID. We lose the ballot. But that kind of proves the point.
Revolutionaries always lose referenda.

He keeps his gloved hand in the air.

But I have doubts about myself.

At a meeting I grandly call for 'the fire, next time.' Where do
I think I am? What do I think I am?

And when I face up to real risk, I bottle it.

There's a minor occupation of the office of the Registrar. And someone has to sit down at his desk, and confront him when he comes in and demands that we all leave. And by now I'm chair of the Socialist Society. But I don't want to do it.

Because I'm fearful that if he told me to get out, I would.

And if I can't do that – sit in someone's chair and not vacate it – what kind of revolutionary am I?

He lowers his fist, and slowly takes off the glove.

My parents weren't involved in the general strike. They weren't miners or from Jewish tailoring stock. They weren't strict or particular. The house wasn't full of Marxist intellectuals.

My grandmother wasn't a suffragette. I wasn't wolf-whistled at. For me, it was never all about the Russians.

My parents first took me to theatre when I was three and three quarters. When I was ten, my dad built a theatre in our garden where me and my friends put on plays.

In February 1969, the same month as the ballot and the Roneo, I am twenty-one. And my parents arrange a dinner in a paneled private room at The Berrow Court Hotel. It's a black tie affair. Mushroom vol-au-vent. Roast duckling. My uncle gives a witty speech. I'd like to say I agreed to go for my parents.

He takes off the glove and looks at it.

And so, what do you do? You realise you have to build a suit of armour to stop you selling out.

He picks up an ancient cassette player. He inserts a cassette.

Commitment, to the working class. Faith, in the ultimate victory of socialism. The certainty, that you hold the key to human history. And the belief that anything that can actually be achieved, in the here and now, is a kind of betrayal of the radiant, post-revolutionary future.

And so you have to join a revolutionary party.

He presses start on the cassette recorder.

Scene Nine: Praxis

DAVID *goes to the microphone. He is now the* OLDER
DAVID. *The* YOUNGER DAVID*'s voice comes out of the
cassette recorder.*

OLDER. Remind me why you didn't?

YOUNGER. What, join?

OLDER. Yes, join.

YOUNGER. I move to Bradford, and become the writer for a
small, Left-wing agitprop theatre group, performing Marxist
plays to workers in struggle. Like, I've made my theory my
practice.

OLDER. Bradford.

DAVID. Yes. Bradford: which, for reasons best known to itself
has won the north of England franchise for the late-sixties
counter-culture, and which plays host to a veritable garden of
exotic theatrical flowers during the two immensely
successful Bradford Festivals of 1970 and 1971.

*He goes and opens cardboard boxes and drawers of filing
cabinets, from which red balloons on ribbons ascend.*

So successful are they, by the by, with so many people
having such an obviously wonderful time, that the city
authorities refuse to finance a third festival, on the grounds
that giving so many people so much unambiguous pleasure
is clearly a gross abuse of public funds.

Performance artists careering around the city on pink
bicycles ridden in aeronautic display formation. Howard
Brenton's play about Scott of the Antarctic being performed
in the city's ice rink, with myself essaying the small but
nonetheless significant role of God. A pagan child's naming
ceremony – with fire-eaters and real goats – in the city's
Wool Exchange.

While a small, stern Marxist theatre troupe, called The
General Will, is presenting the first of a series of agitational
plays which will chart what was effectively a mass uprising
by the industrial working class against the 1970 to 1974
Conservative government, led by Edward Heath. The plays
have heavily ironical titles like *The National Interest* and *The
Dunkirk Spirit*. The last play opens as the government
imposes a three-day working week on all of British industry,
to try and defeat the second miners' strike in two years.

The Prime Minister calls a General Election, on the question
of 'Who governs Britain?'

He loses by a whisker.

And we think: if he'd won, what would the government, the
police, the army, have actually had to do, to defeat the
miners and their allies?

OLDER *uses the mic.* YOUNGER *still comes from the
cassette player.*

OLDER. And you're producing plays.

YOUNGER. We're producing agitprop drama for working-class
audiences.

OLDER. And the form?

YOUNGER. Form?

OLDER. I guess, you'd say, cartoon documentary?

YOUNGER. Oh, *form*. The group favours the documentary
approach because so much information is not presented at all
in the overground media. For instance, the number of factory
sit-ins and occupations which have occurred since 1971. We
list sixty in *State of Emergency*.

OLDER. So it's not about the art.

YOUNGER. No, we're more concerned with what the shows
say than with the aesthetics of how they say it.

OLDER. And what they say isn't about how the personal relates
    to the political. Or prefiguring how a better world might be.
    Or even –

YOUNGER. Look. The Vietnam War's raging. And guess what,
    here, faced with the most determined assault on its rights
    since the general strike, the working class appears to be
    behaving just like Marx and Lenin said it would. So, no, this
    actually isn't the time for prefiguring a better future. Or
    crawling over audiences with no clothes on. Or for that matter
    rapping on about whether there's such a thing as a vaginal
    orgasm. It's for supporting the vanguard of the proletariat in
    what looks increasingly like a battle for state power.

OLDER. And you don't think all this sounds a teeny bit self-
    righteous? From someone who, of course, might become a
    successful professional playwright? Oh, and who thinks
    women's liberation is a distraction from the real struggle?

YOUNGER. I think it's a distraction *now*.

OLDER. And that The General Will will be taken over by a
    faction of its membership, in what you'll call a gay putsch.

DAVID. And, forty-two years later, I'll go back to Bradford to
    find out how a dispute within a tiny theatre group in the
    north of England was actually a microcosm of a struggle
    which was to tear the Left apart: whether the politics of the
    personal – feminism, gay rights – were indeed a distraction
    from the real struggle, or the most important thing that was
    going on.

DUSTY RHODES. *So this is the story of your life, is it?*

DAVID. Dusty Rhodes. Who summarised my version of the
    break-up of The General Will as follows:

    Film of DUSTY RHODES *and* BOBBY WEAVER *is
    projected on the set.*

DUSTY RHODES. *There was a sense of, what you put out, 'I'd
    built a perfectly reasonably company, we were addressing
    the important issues of the day, and then suddenly the*

hippies turned up and it all went to pot, and then the gays took over,' and I thought that was completely dismissive and didn't make sense in terms of what had actually happened.

DAVID. Dusty and Bobby Weaver, members of The General Will.

And Dusty tells me about the last performance of *The Dunkirk Spirit*, which was actually at a fundraiser for the Bradford International Socialists. And how Noël Greig, one of the actors, later co-founder of Gay Sweatshop, had interrupted the performance.

DUSTY RHODES. *The show opened and within a few minutes we got to a point when Noël stepped out on stage dressed up as a captain and he whipped out his Equity card and said: 'As the only Equity card-carrying member of The General Will I'm going on strike, because I'm being oppressed by my heterosexual colleagues.'*

DAVID. Presenting these demands:

VOICE. *We demand: the dissolution of the present General Will theatre company and its reconstitution as a Gay Community Theatre Company.*

DAVID. Which itself provoked protest, from the Bradford Women's Group. Which included Carole Moss and Margaret Robson, also members of The General Will.

Film of MARGARET ROBSON *and* CAROLE MOSS *is projected on the set.*

MARGARET ROBSON. *Hang on a minute? Why is it going to be a gay company? Why isn't it a feminist company?*

DAVID. But the important thing, which I hadn't known about at all, was that neither of these things happened. What did happen was that The General Will issued a call to the alternative arts community of Bradford:

DUSTY RHODES. *If you have anything to say that you would like to say through theatre and community arts, come to The General Will.*

CAROLE MOSS. *There were a lot of Bradford-based gay people, a lot of working-class gay men and women, who became involved, and it was astonishing to see them getting involved in theatre.*

DAVID. Which led to no less than seven shows being performed by community groups under The General Will banner in one year.

CAROLE MOSS. *The Will was trying to follow the debates and struggles that were happening in the world.*

DAVID. And I knew nothing about this.

DUSTY RHODES. *What actually happened was, the working class took over The General Will. We didn't expect they would be lesbians.*

DAVID. But it felt different to the people who were pushed out.

CAROLE MOSS. *I was just angry. My feelings about what happened were coloured by anger all the way through.*

BOBBY WEAVER. *Yes, it was a bit personally threatening to people, certain people were issuing threats.*

MARGARET ROBSON. *We were to be trashed, really, and the language was aggressive, they were going to smash the van...*

DUSTY RHODES. *Do I believe that people were threatened? I daresay that was the case.*

DAVID. But it was part of something that was happening all over.

OLDER. Even, eventually, to me.

MARGARET ROBSON. *I think what happened was that, you know, people involved in the socialist struggle also started to get involved in those waves of feminism, anti-racism, you know, gay politics, which all started to influence and change what people understood to be socialism.*

DAVID. And then the Arts Council took The General Will's grant away.

So they dressed up in carnival costumes with teddy bears and they went down to the Arts Council offices in London, and did a show in the canteen and a protest in the boardroom...

Like they'd done in their protests against the National Front. Costumes and teddy bears and all.

Which had driven the fascists out of Bradford.

Scene Ten: Destiny

OLDER *at the microphone,* YOUNGER *coming from the cassette recorder:*

YOUNGER. And what will I be doing?

OLDER. Writing a play, about the National Front.

YOUNGER. For The General Will?

OLDER. For the Nottingham Playhouse.

YOUNGER. Far out. And what happens?

OLDER. They turn it down.

YOUNGER. That's a pisser.

OLDER. And then you'll rewrite it for the Birmingham Rep, and they'll turn it down.

YOUNGER. Fuckers.

OLDER. And you send it round the country and everybody turns it down, until the Royal Shakespeare Company has second thoughts...

YOUNGER. And?

OLDER....and it goes on at The Other Place at Stratford.

YOUNGER. Which is –

OLDER. A small tin hut in rural Warwickshire.

YOUNGER. Right on.

OLDER. And then they find they have an open slot at the company's West End theatre, the Aldwych.

YOUNGER. So what's this west end play saying?

OLDER. That for all of its claims to the contrary, the National Front was led by, and was a front for, actual Nazis.

YOUNGER. But, hey, doesn't everyone / think that –

OLDER. Which was by no means the prevailing wisdom at the time. And the play is picketed by an offshoot of the National Front who attack the audience with Union Jacks.

And then it goes on television, and it's excellently reviewed by Dennis Potter.

YOUNGER. And speaking of 'the time'...

OLDER. And it makes your – my – our career.

He picks up the cassette player.

YOUNGER. And so you're – I'm – we're, what – in our sixties?

Slight pause.

OLDER. Seventy.

YOUNGER. Wow. Still smoking?

OLDER. No.

YOUNGER. But cooler glasses.

OLDER. More expensive glasses.

YOUNGER. So are you thinking what I'm thinking?

OLDER. Well, that's the question.

Slight pause.

Because by now you've decided that your future was with a different audience, not workers in struggle, but the people that were actually coming to your plays.

And you – I – have understood what I should have learnt at
Bradford, that politics is wider than Marx and Lenin thought
it was, that it expands outward to the planet and inward to
the person, and his or her identity.

Film of ANNA COOTE *is projected on the set.*

ANNA COOTE. *And I wrote, with a friend called Tess Gill, a
book called* Women's Rights: A Practical Guide, *that was
published by Penguin. And we were looking at all the ways,
all the rights that women did and didn't have. So what have
we got, and what do we need?*

DAVID. And Anna finds that when the second edition of the
book was published, they had to almost completely rewrite
it, because so many rights had been won.

ANNA COOTE. *The Sex Discrimination Act,*

OLDER. Tick.

ANNA COOTE. *Changes in the law that enabled women to get
mortgages in their own right,*

OLDER. Tick.

ANNA COOTE. *to sit on juries in their own right,*

OLDER. Tick.

ANNA COOTE. *to have pensions,*

OLDER. Tick.

ANNA COOTE. *women's right to have an income of their own.*

OLDER. Tick.

ANNA COOTE. *And with all those legal advances that we
made, there was the Abortion Act that gave women the right
to choose.*

OLDER *puts down the cassette player.*

OLDER. Tick. In other words, real achievements, in the here
and now.

TARIQ ALI. *I mean, why was the women's movement called the Women's Liberation Movement, clearly linked to the struggle of the third world against the empire? The Gay Liberation Movement, the Black Liberation Movement, the Black Panthers – all these grew up in the late sixties and most of the seventies and they have left their mark.*

YOUNGER. But, hey, I'm writing plays for the Royal Shakespeare Company.

OLDER. But. You'll also write a column on the far-right press for *Searchlight*, which is the leading anti-fascist investigative journal. You'll be a founder member of the Anti-Nazi League. You'll do meetings up and down the country, arguing that the National Front is a Nazi Front. You'll be the most politically active you'll ever be. And the truth is, probably, most of this would not have happened if you hadn't moved into the mainstream.

YOUNGER. Please don't tell me I go into movies.

OLDER. Not yet.

YOUNGER. Move to London?

OLDER. Not on the bucket list so far.

YOUNGER. I don't get a fucking MBE.

OLDER. You don't get a fucking MBE.

YOUNGER. For services to selling out.

OLDER. For services to anything.

YOUNGER. So what's a bucket list?

OLDER. On 3rd May 1979, you'll be in New York, listening to a live relay of the Radio 4 coverage of the General Election result, and the psephologist will refer to the – collapsing – National Front vote as 'the fascist vote'. And you'll feel we've won.

YOUNGER. Far out. And have we?

OLDER. We've won that. But we haven't seen – we haven't understood – what else is happening.

YOUNGER. What am I doing in New York?

OLDER. You're doing what anybody does in a foreign country. You're discovering your own.

Scene Eleven: America

DAVID *picks up his American journal.*

DAVID. In 1976, the bicentennial year of the United States, the British government decides to bestow gifts on a grateful American people. Among them is a scheme to send twenty-five British artists to the States for a year, to do pretty much what they like, perhaps in revenge for the Boston Tea Party. I arrive in November 1978, connect myself to the Manhattan Theatre Club, and spend much of the subsequent twelve months challenging the prevailing myths about the land of the free.

Myth one. Americans don't like queuing. Bollocks. In fact, they all queue all the time. Particularly in banks. You can wait an hour to cash some money or buy travellers cheques. In Britain, there'd be riots.

Myth two. Americans drive big cars fast. Bullshit. They drive big cars incredibly slowly. I'm in America at the height of the late-seventies gas crisis, when the maximum driving speed – this isn't Manhattan, this is on the interstate highway system – is reduced to fifty-five miles an hour and everybody sticks to it and nobody seems to mind.

Myth three. Americans are straight talkers. Baloney. They have a talent for obfuscation, circumlocution and euphemism which would render them the envy of the imperial court of Byzantium.

It is after all in America where I first see the sign: 'Thank you for not smoking.'

An order posing as a courtesy.

'Which major credit card will you be using?': a rule posing as an enquiry.

'Your cooperation is much appreciated': an instruction posing as a prediction implying a threat.

All of which I write down in my journal. Along with witty aphorisms like: 'America, the only country in the world to pass from barbarism to decadence without an intervening period of civilisation.'

And I read it now and I think what a patronising pompous prick I was.

Particularly as the journal lists the people who showered me with friendship, help and hospitality, in New York and Boston, and Los Angeles and San Francisco, and as I travelled all across America.

People of the Left who I want to engage with about what had happened in the sixties.

But also people of the other side, from traditional Republicans to disillusioned working-class Democrats to born-again Christians, who appear to be forming an alarmingly effective coalition to bring the right to power.

The most surprising element of which is to be found in New York, among a group of literary intellectuals, collectively dubbed the Neo-Conservatives, who like to describe themselves as 'liberals mugged by reality'.

Scene Twelve: Defectors

DAVID. The godfather of this movement is Irving Kristol,
   editor of a sober quarterly called *The Public Interest*, and
   author of a book significantly titled *Two Cheers for
   Capitalism*. Kristol identifies a new class of university-
   educated, public-sector employees, which seeks power over
   American business, in alliance with its clients among the
   classes – and indeed races – most dependent on welfare.

   While neo-con Norman Podhoretz, editor of *Commentary*,
   sees feminism and homosexuality as plagues.

   But the reason I go and interview these people is not because
   of their opinions but their history.

   Growing up in poverty in New York City.

   Fighting their way to college.

   Becoming Communists and radicals.

   A photo of IRVING KRISTOL *is projected on the set*.

IRVING KRISTOL. *I suppose the only decision was what kind
   of socialist I would be*.

DAVID. Outraged by the suffering endured by the victims of
   the great depression.

   Inspired by the heroism of the fighters for the Spanish
   Republic.

   But then...

IRVING KRISTOL. *Radical socialism is a version of political
   romanticism*.

DAVID. Disillusioned by Stalin.

IRVING KRISTOL. *All romanticism is vulnerable to reality
   intervening in a shattering way*...

DAVID. Disgusted by apologists for the Soviet Union.

Appalled by the counter-culture of the late sixties.

Moving to the right.

IRVING KRISTOL. *I just grew out of political romanticism.*

DAVID. And so they would support and vote for Ronald
Reagan, as their British equivalents – Alfred Sherman, Paul
Johnson, Kingsley Amis – would support and vote for
Margaret Thatcher.

And as I pack up to come home, I realise what the next play
has to be about.

He puts the journal down.

Scene Thirteen: The Fear

DAVID. But I'm not sure anyone has understood what's
happening. I think we think, 'This is our time.' That as the
economy goes into freefall, everything will fall apart, and
true socialism will emerge like a phoenix from the ashes.
After the deluge, us. So we don't spot the forging of this new
alliance of the so-called producers of society, for aspiration
and ambition but also discipline and authority. The most
lethal cocktail of them all. Which is exactly what it will
prove to be.

OLDER *on the microphone,* YOUNGER *on tape.*

YOUNGER. What do you mean?

OLDER. What do I mean, / what?

YOUNGER. What it proved to be? Is that 'cocktail' not
inherently / unstable –

OLDER. Unstable, certainly.

YOUNGER. Not to mention / contradictory –

OLDER. Contradictory.

YOUNGER. Trying to appeal to authoritarians and libertarians / at once –

OLDER. At once.

YOUNGER. Get the state out of the boardroom, keep it in / the bedroom –

OLDER. The bedroom, absolutely.

YOUNGER. Rapping on about individual freedom, when for the vast majority of Tory voters, and Republicans, the problem isn't too little freedom, but / too much.

OLDER. Too much.

YOUNGER. And surely, if they get / elected –

OLDER. Elected, sure, people will / think –

YOUNGER. Think, it'll be like last time, like with / Heath –

OLDER. Heath.

YOUNGER. And the miners will –

OLDER. Come riding to the / rescue.

YOUNGER. Rescue.

OLDER. Like the US / Cavalry –

YOUNGER. Cavalry, and what makes you / think –

OLDER. Think, what makes me / think –

YOUNGER. Think, that it won't happen this time?

OLDER. Because I know it won't. Because however contradictory it seems in theory, the cocktail will make perfect sense in practice. Particularly to people who lived through the strikes of 1978 to 9, the winter of discontent, and who, presented with this cocktail, decide there is no feasible alternative.

YOUNGER. And you thought that?

OLDER. No of course I didn't think that.

YOUNGER. Well, fab –

OLDER. But I might have felt it. Just a little bit.

Like you did.

Scene Fourteen: Workers' Councils

DAVID *takes a bottle of beer from a filing cabinet and knocks off its cap.*

DAVID. It's early 1979. I am sitting in a bar in New York City. I'm talking to a journalist from the London *Times*. He is a member of the Socialist Workers' Party. He is talking wittily and eruditely of the political situation. I've had a few.

DAVID *sits on a cardboard box with his beer.*

I ask him a question. It's just something that's been bothering me. I know of course that Marx didn't give a blueprint of the new society, that the struggle would throw up the new social forms, that it was the height of petit-bourgeois romanticism to try and speculate about how a post-revolutionary democratic international socialist society would work. But between ourselves. Just in broad outline. How does you think you could actually run a United Socialist States of Europe on the basis of workers' councils?

He embarks on a brilliant analysis of the shortcomings of social-democracy, of the essentially undemocratic character of top-down nationalisation, of the craven failure of the post-war Labour government.

Brilliant, I say. That's really clear, and completely persuasive. But, accepting that the social-democratic alternative is a chimera, nonetheless, in broad outline, how would you, realistically, run a United Socialist States of Europe on the basis on workers' councils?

To which he responds with a stunning dissection of the
incompetence and dogmatism of the East European so-called
workers' states, and indeed the inevitability of both, once the
decision had been taken to embark on the inherently doomed
attempt to build socialism in one country.

Well, of course I knew that. But I'd never heard it expressed
so forcefully and so unanswerably. How could anyone think
otherwise. But. Notwithstanding. Just for laughs. Not as a
blueprint. But just an example of how it might be feasible to
run a United Socialist States of Europe on the basis of
workers' councils?

To which he answers: I have no idea.

OLDER *on the microphone,* YOUNGER *on tape.*

OLDER. Well, is that serious?

YOUNGER. What do you mean, serious?

OLDER. Is that a serious position to hold?

YOUNGER. So how's it going?

OLDER. How's what going?

YOUNGER. This play you're writing about political defection.
Is it working?

OLDER. What do you mean, is it working?

YOUNGER. I mean, I assume you're writing this because
you're scared that it might happen to you.

Isn't that right? Uncle?

Clips from World in Action. *We see* DAVE CLARK *on the
1968 demonstration as we hear his voice, twenty years later.*

DAVE CLARK. *I think I was very idealistic, I was quite naive.
I think I was missing out on the good life, and not achieving
very much in so doing.*

*I think anyone who isn't a socialist at twenty doesn't have
much of a heart. If you're still one at forty there's something
wrong with your head.*

QUESTIONER. *Are you attracted to Thatcherism?*

DAVE CLARK. *Yes I am. Yes, I think the country has turned around.*

OLDER. And if that can happen to Dave Clark...

All over. Game's up. Thatcher's won.

For the first time, he sits in the swivel chair.

Scene Fifteen: Fighting Back

Film of PAUL MASON *is projected on the set.*

PAUL MASON. *I never saw a red flag until I went to university. I never heard a socialist slogan in this working-class town until I went to university, but as I'm in university, there's a guy being killed, there's a mass strike, and then Thatcher's in power and there it comes, the target is us, what are we going to do other than fight back.*

DAVID *stands and goes to one of the red balloons.*

OLDER. And she emasculates the trade unions and sells off council houses and Labour goes down to its worst electoral defeat since 1918.

He bursts the balloon.

The first of three. Women set up the peace camp at Greenham Common.

ANNA COOTE. *I think it was about women doing what they felt like they needed to do. Whether it was campaigning against cruise missiles, or...*

SARAH BRAUN. *Going to Greenham once a year, coachloads of women, that was a terrific high.*

OLDER. And the UK still has a stockpile of over a hundred operational nuclear warheads and four Trident submarines.

He bursts a balloon.

And the US can still deploy its nuclear weapons from British soil wherever it wants to. The Left takes over the Greater London Council.

He bursts a balloon.

HILARY WAINWRIGHT. *Well, firstly we were the industry employment group, and we said that fundamental to our work must be a close relationship with the workers of London and the communities of London… It was a shared power really, it was very much like '68 in office.*

YOUNGER. So Greenham. The GLC. The miners. All around you, struggle going on.

It's just not you doing the struggling.

OLDER. And Mrs Thatcher abolishes the GLC in 1984.

He bursts the penultimate balloon.

YOUNGER. Christ I hope I don't end up being you.

OLDER *switches off the tape.*

OLDER. Sorry.

Pause.

DAVID. And the miners do come riding to the rescue. Their strike against pit closures begins in March 1984. And they go down to defeat a year later.

He is about to burst the last balloon, but changes his mind.

And yet. Groups of miners fan out across the country to build support for the strike, particularly in the cities. Meetings, fundraising, food collections. Gays for the Miners. Hindus for the Miners. Children's parties, pantomimes. The evil Scratcher, trying to abolish Christmas. We take two miners' daughters on our Cornish holiday. Infant-school support groups.

Bringing the most homogenous, as well as the most heroic sector of the proletariat together with the multicultural urban

Left, so they could both learn from each other. And you don't judge the impact of something by its outcome.

HILARY WAINWRIGHT. *So we didn't last long enough to put lot of these things into practice… So my approach is more, what can be learnt from the failure or the difficulties, rather than 'it can't be done.'*

Scene Sixteen: Arcadia

DAVID *turns to the audience.*

DAVID. The structural principle of Shakespeare's arcadian comedies – *As You Like It*, *Midsummer Night's Dream*, *Winter's Tale*, *The Tempest* – is much akin to that of the Northern Line, of the London underground.

You live in the city, usually the court, proceeding gently and predictably upward on life's journey, when, suddenly, you face a crisis and a choice. Marriage or love. Imprisonment or flight. Submission or revolt. You can continue on the course mapped out for you or, through choice or circumstance, you turn another way.

Bohemia. The Green World. Magic islands. Mischief, mystery and madness. Things not what they seem. A forest outside Athens. Girls dressed as boys, and even vice versa. Trying It On.

In *The Tempest*, an elderly courtier called Gonzalo, in the false Duke's entourage, stranded on a magic island, suddenly outlines a vision of a social and political utopia. A municipality, on the south bank of the Thames. A peace camp, outside Greenham.

If this was such a play, then its arcadias would be Manchester and Bradford and America.

And then the lines converge and your life joins up again.
And you go back inside, to the court, or city. And perhaps
you marry, or regain your rightful place, or maybe you
become the king.

But maybe, also – this is Shakespeare's point – as you face
life's further choices... you remember what happened in the
forest or on the island.

And your life will never be the same again.

In 1984 I'm thirty-six.

Scene Seventeen: Settlement

DAVID *opens a drawer of a filing cabinet and takes out a*
bucket. It is full of pieces of paper.

DAVID. And, yes, I am pursuing different aims, with different
ambitions, and my life takes a different course.

He takes out pieces of paper, screws them up, and tosses
them towards the audience.

Get married.

Buy a house.

Take out a mortgage.

Possess a tagine.

Have a West End hit.

Lay down a little wine.

Have a Broadway hit.

Write a film even if it's not a hit. *Lady Jane.* Don't look it up.

Grow a beard, give up smoking, read all of George Eliot,
even *Romola.*

Write the lyrics for the B-side of a hit single.

Actually, do look it up. It's Helena Bonham Carter's first film. There's many good things. It's just a bit slow.

Sue Clegg became a lecturer at Leeds Met, and an expert on higher education. She left the Socialist Workers' Party in the 1990s, but remains a socialist.

Projection of SUE CLEGG *on the set.*

SUE CLEGG. *I think we made a difference. And I don't think we would have been in a position to make such a difference were it not for the fact that we were also organised.*

DAVID. She's also very knowledgable about contemporary opera.

Go to contemporary opera.

Make my own sushi.

Do an interview with Sebastian Coe, for *Marxism Today*.

Actually, write quite a lot for *Marxism Today*. Articles on Thatcherism, racism, even Marx. A piece on Live Aid.

Don't go the Edinburgh Festival ever again.

Projections of BRIAN GOODWIN *and* JILL AMBLER *on the set.*

Brian Goodwin was forced out of his factory as a troublemaker, and won a place at the University of Warwick. Where he met Jill Ambler.

JILL AMBLER. *I mean, we were very much against the nuclear family. I lived in a commune, for goodness' sake.*

DAVID. They moved to Birmingham, became teachers, and joined the Labour Party.

Join the Labour Party.

Run a committee room in five local elections.

See my wife Eve elected as the first ever councillor for our ward.

Projection of SARAH BRAUN *on the set.*

Sarah Braun stopped being active in the women's movement in the early 1980s.

SARAH BRAUN. *I went to the women's centre one day and a very young woman who was there, we got into conversation. And she said, 'You're telling me you've got sons, you're married, you live with a man, you ought to leave them all... You're a traitor to the cause.' And that was the last time I was involved.*

DAVID. Sarah still makes banners for trade unions and left-wing causes. I interviewed both her and her husband Ted, former Professor of Drama at Bristol, four days before he died.

Found a postgraduate course in playwriting.

Become a professor.

Write for the *London Review of Books*.

Visit Budapest, Warsaw, Auschwitz. Berlin.

So when it happens, you've been there.

Footage of the fall of the Berlin Wall is projected on the set.

So many plays are written about the fall of Eastern European Communism that it's rumoured Bucharest Airport is opening a special British Playwrights' Lounge.

I write three such plays. Noticing how much of 1989 is an echo of 1968.

Protestors planting flowers behind the shields of the riot police. Chanting 'We Are Your Children' and 'The Whole World Is Watching'. Prague's Lennon wall – Lennon not Lenin. Imagine.

A generation which believes in freedom, justice and emancipation.

And that Margaret Thatcher deserves the Nobel Peace Prize.

And for the new millennium:

Be on *Any Questions*.

Get invited on to *Desert Island Discs*.

Start drawing up your list immediately. 'Street Fighting Man'. 'Subterranean Homesick Blues'. 'Imagine'.

Debate at the Oxford Union.

Pause.

Dining in college.

Mastering watercolour.

Living in a cathedral close.

Or Umbria.

Or in Cornwall, by the sea.

Delete 'Street Fighting Man'. Insert 'Fantasia on a Theme by Thomas Tallis'.

Maybe keep 'Imagine'.

In July 1997 my wife Eve is diagnosed with lung cancer. She dies the following March. She told her sons – now my sons – Sean and Nigel she wanted me to find someone else, as indeed I do. And Steph's a playwright, and we write two plays together, one of them a community play for Dorchester. And she was on the women's demonstration against Trump, and she's angrier than I am, and you could argue that she lives her politics more than I do now, or perhaps I ever have.

Don't buy from Amazon.

Don't eat anything with a face.

Or anywhere that is, or is owned by, McDonald's.

No plastic in the house.

And talking of things you can actually do...

He takes a document from the bucket. We don't know what it is. The 'ticks' are projected on the set.

Minimum wage.

Tick.

Fuel allowance for pensioners.

Tick.

Minister for Women.

Tick.

More support for victims of rape.

Tick.

Remove discrimination against homosexuals.

Tick.

Introduce a Scottish Assembly.

Tick.

Establish a devolved administration in Northern Ireland.

Tick.

Establish a Ministry of Overseas Development.

Tick.

Increase overseas aid to nought-point-seven per cent.

Tick.

Introduce a Freedom of Information Bill.

Tick.

Abolish hunting with dogs.

Tick.

He looks at the front of the document.

Oh. The Labour Party Manifesto, 1983. The proverbial
longest suicide note in history. Economic policies: wealth
tax, rent freeze, national investment bank: cross cross cross.
But women's rights, tick. Gay rights, tick. International aid,

devolution, freedom of information, tick tick tick tick tick tick. The exemplar of rampant Left impossibilism. Crashing to historic electoral defeat. Now the common sense of the age. The red lines of the culture war. The war we won.

Scene Eighteen: Revolution

DAVID. A month after Eve is diagnosed, we're turning out of the car park of a hotel in Oxford, where we'd stayed the night. We turn on the car radio and hear someone talking sepulchrally about what was obviously a dead royal. Ah, we think, that's the Queen Mother.

A week later, Eve's sister and her family are visiting, but I still insist on watching Diana's funeral.

The Royal Family, not knowing what the fuck had hit them.

Hyde Park, full of a rainbow nation. Old-young, black-white, gay-straight. The victors in the culture war.

The way the applause after Earl Spencer's speech rolled into Westminster Abbey, like thunder, from the streets.

A floral revolution, like Greenham, like Prague in 1989, like San Francisco in 1967.

And thinking about other funerals that became acts of rebellion and defiance. Steve Biko in South Africa. The night-time funerals in Gaza.

And actually, that strange alliance between jet-set celebrity and the wretched of the earth which gave us Live Aid?

Which my son Sean attends. And it's far out. And although this is not a universally accepted truth, for me, it is actually a celebration of collective action, of people working together for the good of others, in however small a way, for all mankind, like the Free Mandela concert would be, an affirmation, actually, of the importance of charity, because, actually, that's where you start, with the charitable impulse, isn't it? Even if that isn't where / you end –

DANNI. I'm sorry, I – I'm sorry, I just can't.

DAVID *doesn't know what's happening. He tries to restart.*

DAVID. Um. Steve Biko, in South Africa –

DANNI. I mean, for Christ's sake, *Mandela*.

DAVID. Is everything okay?

DANNI. Is everything *okay*?

DANNI *shuts the show laptop, disabling the tech.* DAVID *can't say anything.*

And Steve Biko is the same as, like, Diana? Princess Diana? Wasn't she the woman who spent twenty-five grand a year on fucking underwear? And wasn't Live Aid actually thirty multi-millionnaires in the greatest act of virtue-signaling in history? And actually, yes, Bob, they do know it's Christmas, most Africans are Christians. So, no Bob, and actually, Bob, Muslim kids die too. So I just can't. And I mean I'm sorry, you've all paid money, but I can't, you just can't say 'little yellow people' or girls passing hands across men's brows, or 'mankind', for fuck's sake, however much it's all in quote marks, and you always say, like it's quote marks, they'll get it's quote marks. And have I got this right, the National Front was defeated by *your play*?

DAVID. No, I'm obviously –

DANNI. And I'm sorry, I know how important this is for you, I know you've done like important shit and it's what you've always wanted, but still – day after day. And you're saying, it's the cynical, and pessimistic, oh, we did it all and no one else has a right to be active or be angry because it was all done in the sixties and we're like living in your fucking wake.

DAVID. Of course I don't / think –

DANNI. And tell me, 'feminism was a distraction', are we supposed, I mean, do you want a fucking medal for not

thinking that any more? That's if you don't? And 'we won
the culture war'. Well let's just unpick 'we'. And 'won'.
And what about the war you lost? Or like not bothered
fighting?

DAVID. What / war –

DANNI. The one waged against me? Hashtag
theworkingclassinfuckingstruggle? I don't need charity, I
need a rent freeze.

DAVID. But the next / thing I –

DANNI. But ooh you're a baby boomer and you're sitting on a
million quid's worth of prime real estate and whoo-hoo you
won gay rights. And if this is a play, then who's it for?

DAVID *is devastated.*

Because please, please not 'Imagine'. No possessions.
Really? You? So are we discussing property? So I'm sorry.
Fuck. End of thing. Exit. Sorry.

DANNI *goes out. The autocue has been disabled:* DAVID
doesn't know what to do. He goes to DANNI*'s desk. He looks
hopelessly at the laptop. He presses a button.
Incomprehensible hieroglyphs appear on the set. He has no
idea at all.*

Scene Nineteen: Winning the War

DAVID *picks up the prompt book in its big, heavy ring file. He
turns to the audience and delivers his next speech.*

DAVID *(finding his place)*. Um… So. Diana's funeral. And we
won the culture war.

But while it was being won, yes, we lost the other war, the
war against what had first been called monetarism, then
Thatcherism, then Neo-liberalism, and now austerity.

He realises he has to read out a clip.

And Martin Jacques says: 'In a way, I think Thatcher saw it as her final victory, that the Labour Party capitulated to neo-liberalism.'

And I say: 'And of course abandoning the people who had the right to think that someone would stand up for them.'

And then suddenly, against all our expectations, there was the crash.

There was a sound effect here, which he has to find a way of doing. He drops the bucket on the floor.

And for the next ten years, real income would decline, and debt would climb, particularly for people in their twenties and their thirties.

And yes of course there were the anti-globalisation protesters, and in 2011 Occupy Wall Street, and the Day X protestors against student fees, and Occupy tent city outside Paul's Cathedral… and that summer there were the riots, and the Spanish Indignados and the Greek uprising and that spring, the Arab Spring.

But actually, for eight years, there was no serious force in mainstream politics putting forward an alternative. And Paul Mason says:

'And in the end, if you don't put forward an alternative, somebody else will.'

Then he realises the problem with the next section.

Survey.

Scene Twenty: New Fault Line

DAVID *gets a thick magic marker from* DANNI*'s desk. He gets the survey clipboard out of its filing cabinet.*

DAVID. Now. Imagine. You're a graduate, working in the public sector or the creative industries, a teacher or a local-government employee. Perhaps a student. Maybe the sort of person who likes to go to the theatre of an evening. Do you agree or disagree with the following propositions?

As he speaks, he writes a list on the set: 'CIVIL LIBS, FREE MARKET, IMM, LESS TAX'. Then he'll put ticks on one side and crosses on the other. He solicits answers from the audience.

Immigration is a benefit not a burden to society. People like you, for heaven's sake. (*Yes.*)

The freer the market, the freer the people. (*No.*)

Civil liberties are just as important as national security. (*Yes.*)

Corporations and rich people should pay less tax. (*No.*)

Now imagine you're a dotcom billionaire or a Hollywood mogul or star.

He puts ticks down one side.

Immigration is a benefit not a burden. All those Hungarian film editors. (*Yes.*)

Free market, free people. If you're honest. (*Yes.*)

Civil liberties are just as important as national security. (*Yes.*)

Corporations and rich people should pay less tax. (*Yes.*)

Re-enter DANNI.

Now you're a fifty-five-year-old unemployed white plumber in Burnley.

He puts crosses down the other side.

Immigration is a benefit. (*No*.)

Free market, free people. (*No*.)

Civil liberties are just as important as national security. (*No*.)

Corporations and rich people should pay less tax. Than you. (*No*.)

He draws a thick black line between Hollywood and Burnley.

A new fault line, with economic and social liberalism on one side, and social conservatism and economic intervention on the other.

Which is why, from Warsaw to Wisconsin, right-wing populist parties moved their economic programmes to the left, from Poland's Law and Justice Party, suddenly embracing welfare, to Donald Trump promising the biggest programme of public works since the 1930s.

And why the majority of my generation voted Brexit. Because the California dreaming of the 1960s turned out to be just that. Because they felt let down and left behind. By a magical mystery tour which never arrived. And so the generation that came of age in the 1960s tried to turn the clock back to their childhoods.

DANNI. And of course you know all about what Burnley plumbers think of tax and immigration.

Pause.

DAVID. No, the point is –

DANNI. I know the point.

Slight pause.

DAVID. So, you're…

DANNI. I'm not standing here saying sorry.

DAVID. No.

Pause. Then DANNI *goes to* DAVID *and takes the book from him.*

DANNI. Oh, for fuck's sake. Give me that. You can't even learn it.

She sees her magic marker, picks it up and takes that and the book back to her desk.

And you've written all over the set.

She sits, looks at the script.

Where are you?

DAVID. 'Re-enter the Stage Manager.'

DANNI*'s about to restart the autocue. Then she changes her mind.*

DANNI. So. Diana died when I was two. What have you been doing in my lifetime?

DAVID. Well –

DANNI. Apart from brushing up the watercolour.

DAVID. Well, I've kept on writing the plays.

DANNI. About?

DAVID. Conflict resolution, multiculturalism, Nazi Germany, the English Bible –

DANNI. And no doubt some book reviews.

DAVID. Yes, and articles, I've spoken, actually quite a lot, at meetings –

DANNI. Stop the war.

DAVID. Stop the war, and anti-racism, and I've done some good stuff for the union –

DANNI. Whoo-hoo.

DAVID. Well, yes, whoo-hoo, and defending playwrights from the idea that what we do is inherently undemocratic and hierarchical and authoritarian –

DANNI. Author. Authority.

DAVID. Well, that's how they put it, certainly. And I actually /
run a charity –

DANNI. And your friends have kept the faith and they think
their young self would be proud of them.

DAVID. Hilary Wainwright thinks her younger self would be
appalled that she joined the Labour Party. And moved to
London.

DANNI. And?

DAVID. And Martin Jacques thinks that *Marxism Today* should
have done more on racism and equality. And that the most
important events of the last century were the Chinese
revolution and decolonisation, which are transforming the
world.

DANNI. Yet you still think you haven't done enough to bring
about the change that you believe in.

DAVID. No.

DANNI. But the thing you're really frightened of, is you
haven't done enough to stop the things you don't believe in.

DAVID. Yes.

DANNI. Euro pop-right Brexit.

DAVID. Trump. And, as a result, we may lose all the gains
we've made.

DANNI. So what do I think?

DAVID. What do you think?

DANNI. Thanks for asking. I think it was a night in June last
year, and we had a cardboard cutout of this old bloke, and
three bottles of prosecco. One for each million extra votes he
won. With a radical economic manifesto. Loads working-
class. Most young. What's the sixties slogan about age?

DAVID. 'Don't trust anybody over thirty.'

DANNI. Well, now most people don't vote Tory till they're
forty-seven. And if I was – (*Gesture at cassette player.*) him,

and I knew what you know now, I'd ask you this. If none of
this had happened. If Lehman Brothers had done a risk
assessment. If David Milliband was Prime Minister. If it was
still economics nil and culture fab and cool and far out and
right on. If your generation's legacy was only sex and drugs
and rock'n'roll. Deep Down. Would you really mind?

DAVID. Okay. Could you...?

Scene Twenty-One: The V&A

DANNI *reactivates the tech, including the autocue*. DAVID *to
the audience*.

DAVID. It's the 16th of February 2017. In preparation for
writing this show, I go to the Victoria and Albert museum to
see an exhibition about the sixties called 'You Say You Want
a Revolution?, which is of course the first line of 'Revolution
1' the first track on side four of the Beatles' White Album,
recorded on 30th May 1968.

They point out that the contraceptive pill wasn't available to
single women before 1968.

But LSD was legal.

There's a bit about the Panthers. There's a lot about the
Beatles.

And the exhibition draws a direct line from all of that to
Steve Jobs and the Mac computer. From Swinging London to
Silicon Valley. Apple to Apple.

Apparently he said that the *Whole Earth Catalog* was 'sort of
like Google in paperback form'.

The thesis: the only thing the sixties did for us was
individual freedom. Its enduring legacy not socialism but a
renewal of capitalism.

'I'd like to buy the world a fucking Coke.'

Oh, yes. Yes. I really mind.

Scene Twenty-Two: 70/20 Survey

Suddenly, DANNI *goes to the audience.*

DANNI. Alright. Who's over forty-seven?

They vote.

Okay, then. You. Hands up who believed the following at twenty:

Marriage should be abolished as a legal status.

No industries should be privately owned for profit.

There should be no restrictions on immigration.

Which of you believes all of those things now? At least one of them?

Now, all those under forty-seven. Hands up those who believe these things now.

Everyone should have the right to choose their gender and act on that decision.

All companies should be coops owned and run by their workers.

There should be no border controls between countries.

Who thinks they'll still believe all of these things at seventy? At least one of them?

(*To* DAVID.) See? (*Or:*) Fine.

She goes and gets a pile of cards from a filing cabinet.

Now imagine. It's 2048. He's a hundred. I'm fifty-three. Almost everybody's over forty-seven.

Who can bear to think that any of the following might still not have been achieved?

She hands DAVID *a pile of cards.*

Scene Twenty-Three: Final Audit

The first card reads: 'MANIFESTO OF THE LABOUR PARTY, 2017.'

DAVID. Abolition of university tuition fees.

Banning of zero-hours contracts.

DANNI *hands piles of programmes to the audience.*

DANNI. Can you pass these round, please? It's the programme.

DAVID *drops the first card, revealing the next card: 'JOHN LENNON: 'IMAGINE', 1988.'*

DAVID. Imagine there's no countries. It isn't hard to do.

'MANIFESTO OF THE LABOUR PARTY, 1983.'

The ending of all forms of academic selection.

DANNI. Please don't read the programme now.

DAVID. Cancellation of Trident.

'PROGRAMME OF THE BLACK PANTHER PARTY, 1966.'

We Want Freedom. We Want Power To Determine The Destiny Of Our Black Community.

(*Prompts* DANNI.) We want Education –

DANNI. We Want Education That Teaches Us Our True History and Our Role In The Present-Day Society.

'UNIVERSAL DECLARATION OF HUMAN RIGHTS, 1948.'

DAVID. Slavery and the slave trade shall be prohibited in all their forms.

DANNI. No one shall be subjected to arbitrary interference with his privacy, family, home or correspondence.

'EQUAL RIGHTS AMENDMENT, 1943.'

DAVID. Equality of rights under the law shall not be denied or abridged by the United States or by any State on account of sex.

DANNI. Still not ratified.

'COMMUNIST MANIFESTO, 1848.'

DAVID. Abolition of all rights of inheritance.

DANNI. National bank with exclusive monopoly.

'ACT II, SCENE I, THE TEMPEST, 1611.'

DAVID. I' the commonwealth I would by contraries
Execute all things; for no kind of traffic
Would I admit; no name of magistrate;
Riches, poverty,
And use of service, none.

'ST MATTHEW'S GOSPEL, WILLIAM TYNDALE NEW TESTAMENT, 1526.'

DANNI. Blessed are the meek: for they shall inherit the earth.

DAVID *drops the last card.*

DAVID. To bring about a fundamental and irreversible shift in the balance of power and wealth in favour of working people and their families.

DANNI. Contract, succession,
Bourn, bound of land, tilth, vineyard, none;

DAVID. Everyone has the right to form and to join trade unions.

DANNI. No sovereignty;

DAVID. Everyone, without any discrimination, has the right to equal pay for equal work.

DANNI. Prohibit unauthorised surveillance.

DAVID *gets the only unburst balloon*.

We Want An Immediate End To Police Brutality And Murder Of Black People.

DAVID. No one shall be subjected to arbitrary arrest, detention or exile.

DAVID *hands* DANNI *the balloon and leaves the stage*.

DANNI. But nature should bring forth
Of its own kind, all foison, all abundance,
To feed my innocent people.

We Want Land, Bread, Housing. Education, Clothing, Justice And Peace.

I would with such perfection govern, sir,
To excel the golden age.

If this is a play,

This is the ending.

Trying It On was commissioned by Warwick Arts Centre and produced by China Plate theatre studio. It was first performed at Warwick Arts Centre on 7 June 2018, at the beginning of a tour which included dates at the Birmingham Repertory Theatre; the Midlands Arts Centre, Birmingham; the Royal Shakespeare Company's Other Place Theatre, Stratford-upon-Avon; and the Royal Court Theatre Upstairs, London.

Creative Team

David Edgar	*Writer and Performer*
Christopher Haydon	*Director*
Frankie Bradshaw	*Designer*
William Reynolds	*Lighting and Video Designer*
Ella Wahlström	*Sound Designer*
Anna Poole	*Assistant Director*
Kady Howey Nunn	*Production Manager*
Danielle Phillips	*Stage Manager*
Alex Johnston	*Deputy Production Manager*
Jade Nagi	*Deputy Stage Manager*
Dave Pinnegar	*Technician*
Tim Brieley	*Set Builder*
Catherine Dale	*Transcriptions*

Interviews filmed by

Rachel Bunce, Justin Jones and Brett Chapman

Research and Development Collaborators

Lu Kemp, Oliver Townsend, Matt Regan, Alex Austin, Helen Mugridge, Chris Thorpe, Francesca Millican-Slater and Stephanie Ridings

Christopher Haydon | Director

Christopher Haydon was artistic director of the Gate Theatre from 2012–2017, where his productions included the UK premiere of *The Convert* by Danai Gurira, and his award-winning world-premiere production of *Grounded* by George Brant, which toured nationally and internationally. Recent freelance directing credits include: *On the Exhale* (China Plate/Traverse Theatre, Winner: Fringe First Award); *The Caretaker* (Bristol Old Vic/Royal and Derngate Northampton); *Twelve Angry Men* (Birmingham REP/West End). His first short film *In Wonderland* was funded by Film London and is currently playing at festivals around the world.

Danielle Phillips | Stage Manager

Danielle Phillips graduated from LAMDA in 2016 with a BA (Hons) degree in Professional Acting. Theatre includes: *Dark Winter* (Hull Truck); *Reared* (Theatre503); *E15* (Lung Theatre and Battersea Arts Centre); *The 56* (Lung Theatre and Battersea Arts Centre, for which she was awarded the Most Promising award at the National Student Drama Festival in 2015); *Istanbul: You'll Never Walk Alone* (From the Gut Theatre); *The Flood* (National Youth Theatre). Film includes: *Ready Player One*.

Frankie Bradshaw | Designer

Frankie Bradshaw was a Jerwood Young Designer in 2017, the winner of the OffWestEnd Best Set Design award in 2016, and was a Linbury Prize finalist in 2015. She has designed across the UK in venues including Theatre Royal Haymarket, Young Vic, Royal Exchange, Manchester, The Watermill Theatre, Salisbury Playhouse and the Gate Theatre.

William Reynolds | Lighting and Video Designer

William Reynolds is Artistic Director of Metta Theatre (www.mettatheatre.co.uk) and an Artist in Residence at the

V&A Museum. Recent set and lighting design credits include: *Weimar Cabaret* (Barbican); *Sonnet Walks* (Globe Theatre); *Little Mermaid* (Theatre by the Lake and UK tour); *Radiant Vermin* (Soho Theatre and Brits Off-Broadway). Upcoming designs include: *In the Willows* (Exeter Northcott and UK tour) and *Pictures of Dorian Gray* (Jermyn Street Theatre).

Ella Wahlström | Sound Designer

Ella Wahlström is a London-based sound designer. She studied violin in Finland and trained as a Theatre Sound Designer at Rose Bruford College, London. Credits include: original sound operator of Complicité's *The Encounter*; sound designer for Esa-Pekka Salonen's cello concerto; Mischief's *Peter Pan Goes Wrong*; and Robert Wilson and Mikhail Baryshnikov's *Letter to a Man*.

Anna Poole | Assistant Director

Anna Poole was recently the Jerwood Assistant Director on *Wings* (Young Vic). Other assistant directing credits include: *Bordergame* (National Theatre Wales); *Gary's Mobile Disco* (Waking Exploits, Chapter Arts Centre); *Last Christmas* (Dirty Protest, Edinburgh Festival Fringe). Her directing credits include: *Opera Scenes* (RWCMD); *Signs/Wonders* by Katherine Soper (Five Plays, Young Vic).

Kady Howey Nunn | Production Manager

Kady Howey Nunn is a production manager who has most recently worked with China Plate, Complicité, Clean Break, Young Vic, and the National Theatre. Production management credits include: *Everything That Rises Must Dance* (A Dance Umbrella and Complicité production); *La Voix Humaine* (Opera Up Close at Kings Place); *The Lounge* (Soho Theatre); *So It Goes* (Shanghai Arts Fest).

Warwick Arts Centre, situated on the campus of the University of Warwick, is one of the largest multi-artform venues in the UK. Since it opened in 1974, the Arts Centre has been a distinctive special place, integral to university life, an important resource for the arts and for audiences in the region and a significant force in national and international arts networks.

China Plate is an independent theatre studio that works with artists, venues, festivals and funders to challenge the way performance is made, who it's made by and who gets to experience it. They are Associate Producers at Warwick Arts Centre. China Plate are Ed Collier, Paul Warwick, Rosie Kelly, Andrea Pierides, Tamara Moore, Sarah-Jane Watkinson, Sarah Isaacs and Vikesh Godhwani.

A Nick Hern Book

Maydays & Trying It On first published as a paperback original in Great Britain in 2018 by Nick Hern Books Limited, The Glasshouse, 49a Goldhawk Road, London W12 8QP

Maydays copyright © 1984, 2018 David Edgar
Trying It On copyright © 2018 David Edgar
Introduction copyright © 2018 David Edgar

An earlier version of *Maydays* was published by Methuen Drama in 1984. The play is published here by permission of Bloomsbury Methuen Drama, an imprint of Bloomsbury Publishing Plc.

David Edgar has asserted his right to be identified as the author of these works

Front cover image © RSC
Back cover image © Warwick Arts Centre / China Plate

Designed and typeset by Nick Hern Books, London
Printed in Great Britain by Mimeo Ltd, Huntingdon, Cambridgeshire PE29 6XX

A CIP catalogue record for this book is available from the British Library

ISBN   978 1 84842 732 7

www.nickhernbooks.co.uk

facebook.com/nickhernbooks

twitter.com/nickhernbooks